HG4553.L68
LOW   23
UNDERSTANDING THE
STOCK MARKET

Understanding the Stock Market

A GUIDE FOR

UNDERSTANDING

BOSTON · TORONTO

YOUNG INVESTORS

the STOCK MARKET

by JANET LOW

LITTLE, BROWN and COMPANY

PREFACE

The late C. F. Kettering, who was for many years an executive of General Motors, once said, "I object to people running down the future. I am going to live the rest of my life there, and I'd like it to be a nice place." Amen to that.

Many people who share Mr. Kettering's feeling have discovered that one way of helping to make the future "a nice place" may be to put some of today's money to work in the hope of enjoying tomorrow some of the necessities, comforts, and luxuries that money can buy. In other words, to buy securities.

Investing in stocks and bonds does not, of course, guarantee profits. Nevertheless, in the fifteen years from 1952 to 1967, the number of Americans owning stocks increased almost four-fold — from 6,490,000 to 24,000,000. It stands to reason that the number would not have increased greatly if many people had not found investing in stocks and bonds profitable.

The number of stockholders in the country will probably multiply again as more and more young people come of age and decide to buy stocks and bonds for themselves. It is to give them an understanding of the market and the way it works that this book was written. The book is for novices, not for sophisticates.

Every effort has been made to ensure the accuracy of the information in this book. I would like to thank many friends in Wall Street who gave me help in various forms, including Jane Neville, who typed the manuscript. And special thanks go to my young friends Sally Tonkin, Paul Chironis, Steven Chironis, and Christian Doherty, who read the manuscript and made many helpful suggestions.

Janet Low

CONTENTS

ix

CONTENTS

Understanding the Stock Market

Understanding the Stock Market

INTRODUCTION

If a visitor from another country or another planet arrived at your house and started to ask you questions about "the American way of life," you would undoubtedly tell him about the Constitution and the Bill of Rights, about how government officials are elected, about freedom of speech and of the press and of assembly — in short, about democracy as it is practiced in the United States.

But what if the visitor were to ask you about our economic system — about where the money comes from that keeps the country going? You would have to tell him about our free-enterprise system and explain that despite its name, it actually involves a great deal of money, which is called capital. That is what this book is about: money or capital and where it comes from and how it is used to keep the factories going and the country prospering.

There is an old saying, "The best things in life are free." And so they are. But don't take that old saying too literally. The *best* things are free, but *everything* isn't free. Good health is free, but when you're sick, doctors and hospitals and medicines cost money. Fresh air is free, but it is costing us more every year to eliminate the air pollution caused by automobiles and factories. And food, clothing, and shelter are not free, as you know. In short, *you* can't get along without money, and neither can the government and industry.

Money is usually defined as a medium of exchange or a measure of value. It is both, of course. And it is something else as well. It is the lifeblood of the nation — not its bones and organs, not its brain, but the substance that nourishes them all. This book doesn't tell the whole story of money — not by any means. But it may give you an idea of what to say to your visitor from another country if he should arrive.

One more thing. This book is a little bit like a jigsaw puzzle. You may find it hard at first because the pieces will seem to have very little to do with one another. But after a while, a pattern will emerge. And when you have finished, all the pieces will fit.

1.

Fundamentals First

Before you can play a game, you have to know what the rules are and what the terms mean. With baseball, for example, you have to know the number of men on a team, what a diamond is, the meaning of ball and strike, and how the game is scored.

In the same way, before you can understand the American economic system, you have to know what the rules are and what the terms mean.

Take the word *economics,* for example. To the ancient

Greeks, who invented the word, it meant the management of a household. Later it was extended to mean the management of a whole country — the way it gets its money, the way it spends its money, the way it uses its natural resources, everything that has to do with the country's financial condition.

A Word About Systems

Then there's the word *capitalism*. Ours is a capitalistic country. That means that private citizens — not government — run industry and market goods in competition with other private citizens doing the same thing. And the people who keep the businesses going get the profits — if there are any — and pay taxes to the government to keep it running.

When you have lived all your life in a country with a capitalistic system, it may be hard to imagine any other. But capitalism is not the only system there is. For example, many countries all over the world operate according to an economic system called socialism. In a socialistic country, the government (rather than private citizens) owns and controls industry and markets goods and distributes profits as it sees fit. Communism is a form of socialism and was described by its founder this way: "From each according to his abilities, to each according to his needs." In other words, everyone is expected to work to his capacity, and the proceeds from everybody's work are divided according to each person's need rather than his contribution as a worker. Or as the nineteenth-century writer Ebenezer Elliott put it: "What is a communist? One who has yearnings / For equal division of unequal earnings."

Perhaps an example will make clearer the difference between the two most widespread economic systems in the world today, capitalism and socialism. When you were a youngster, probably you had a lemonade stand at some time. Why? Primarily to make money. Operating under a capitalistic system, you set up a stand and made lemonade and sold it to the neighbors. And you were allowed to keep your profits for your own use.

But suppose you lived under a socialistic system. In the first place, you wouldn't own your own lemonade stand. The government would own it and employ you to run it. And you would not be allowed to pocket any profits. You would have to turn them in to the government, which would put them with the profits from other businesses and then give back to you (and others) what it considered enough money to live on — or enough so that when it was added to the rest of your family's income, it would provide living expenses for all of you.

These descriptions are much oversimplified, of course. In practice, our capitalistic system has been moving toward socialism in recent years. Our move toward socialism seems to come from the realization that even though many people prosper in our capitalistic country, there are many others who cannot seem to make a living and who need help from those who can through the government.

Interestingly enough, some socialistic countries have been moving toward capitalism at the same time, perhaps because they recognize the fact that socialism does not provide much incentive for doing good work, since the worker does not benefit in proportion to his contribution and does not enjoy the fruits of his own labors. Thus two men working side by side in a factory may get paid exactly the same amount of money, even though one does good, careful, fast work and the other is slow and careless. Those countries are moving also toward a system that gives greater emphasis to marketing — to satisfying the needs and wants of their citizens instead of simply manufacturing and offering only what the government thinks people should have. Thus the socialists are beginning to recognize the fact that people's wants are not all the same and are moving to make their economic system more flexible.

For better or for worse, each system — capitalism as well as communism — seems to be influenced by the other to some extent.

The Law of the Land

There is another kind of interrelationship that exists in all kinds of economic systems. It is called the law of supply and demand. In its simplest form, it means that at any given time, the amount of a product that is available (the supply) tends to seek a balance with the amount of the product that people want (the demand). For example, if all the stores in your neighborhood suddenly have lots of apples on hand — more apples than their customers want to buy — the chances are that one store and then another and then another will try to create a bigger demand for apples by lowering the price. Similarly, if there were a shortage of apples, you might expect the price of the few available apples to be relatively high. Price is a way of helping supply and demand reach a balance.

In practice, the law of supply and demand is almost never allowed to work freely without some interference, usually by the government. Governments have many ways of affecting the balance of supply and demand, some of them subject to a great deal of argument and disagreement. In the United States, the federal government reduces the size of the country's wheat crop by paying some farmers *not* to grow wheat and by buying some wheat itself and using it to feed the hungry at home and abroad. Keeping the supply of wheat and the demand for wheat in balance also keeps the price profitable to farmers and reasonable to consumers — in theory, at least. Thus the government tries to prevent the kind of imbalance that we just mentioned in connection with apples.

Tinkering with the Economy

The government also has ways of influencing the supply and demand of money. You may have thought of money only as a medium of exchange, a means of buying and selling. But it is actually a commodity like wheat in some respects. A group of seven men called the Federal Reserve Board, appointed by the President and confirmed by the Senate, has the power to increase or decrease the amount of money in circulation at any given time. It has a number of ways of doing this, one being the regulation of the interest rate, the amount of money that it costs to borrow money, the amount of interest that a borrower must pay to use money for a while. When money is in short supply ("tight," as the economists put it), it costs more to borrow it. When there is plenty of money available (when money is "easy"), it costs less to borrow it. The law of supply and demand again. And don't think for a minute that the amount of money in circulation has nothing to do with you and your family. It affects the amount of interest you get on a savings account in a bank. It affects the cost of buying a house or a car, since most people pay for such purchases over a period of time and pay interest on the unpaid balance of money they owe until it is all paid off. It affects the amount of money that is available for new buildings and for expansion of factories and for all kinds of growth and development. Sooner or later, it affects virtually everything in the national economy. But more of that later.

2.

Capitalism and How It Works

Let's go back to that lemonade stand that you had when you were six or seven. Your parents and the neighbors probably praised you for your enterprise and told you that you were "a real little businessman" or "a real little capitalist." But were you? Well, yes and no. You understood the profit motive; you had a product to sell and some knowledge of your market, the people who might buy your product; and you may even have had some competition — another lemonade stand in the neighborhood.

Capitalism Without the Capital

But what you probably didn't have was capital. Very likely your mother gave you the lemons and sugar and paper cups you needed, and perhaps the local grocery store supplied the crates to make the stand. So for all your enterprise, you didn't have to face the basic problem of capitalism: capital and how to raise it, money to start a business venture. Someone had to pay for the lemons and sugar. Someone always has to pay for the lemons and sugar — or whatever raw materials are needed and whatever facilities are required to start a business.

After childhood, it is not Father who supplies the necessary money, nor is it the government. It is capitalists. And who are capitalists? They are people who have put money aside after paying their living expenses, people who have what economists call "accumulated wealth," a little or a lot. They may have worked for that money or inherited it or invested money and seen it grow. However they acquired it, it is capital and they are capitalists. The word capitalist used to be applied only to people with a great deal of money. But as there were fewer and fewer very rich people (partly because of the graduated income tax) and more and more moderately rich people, the word came to be used for anyone who had money to spare after paying the cost of living.

What Is a Dollar Worth?

What do capitalists do with their capital after they have acquired it? In our country, whatever they please. Some put it away in a cookie jar or teapot or under the mattress — all bad places for money, by the way, not just because it may be stolen

11

but also because its purchasing power may decline as prices rise. You may say that a dollar is always worth 100 cents in good times and bad, and that is true. But it won't always buy the same amount of merchandise. A loaf of bread which cost about ten cents during the 1930's costs about thirty cents in the 1960's. A quart of milk has risen about the same amount. Houses and automobiles have increased to several times what they used to cost. Except during certain relatively brief periods of financial crisis, throughout the history of our country, prices have tended to go up and the purchasing power of the dollar — the amount that the dollar will buy — has tended to go down. Since World War II, purchasing power has declined about 3 percent a year. So if you put your money in a cookie jar for five years and then take it out to buy something, you'll probably find that the price of the thing you want has gone up and therefore your money will buy less of it or will buy something of lower quality than it would have bought five years before.

Magic at Work

What about putting that extra money in a bank? It's safe there; that's pretty certain. And a bank will pay interest on your money — $4\frac{1}{2}$ or 5 percent a year. That means that if you put $100 in a bank that pays 5 percent interest and leave it there, at the end of the first year you'll have $105. And at the end of the second year, you'll have $110 — right? Wrong. You'll have $110.25. That's because the bank will pay interest not only on the amount you deposited ($100), which is called the principal, but also on the interest that has accumulated ($5 the first year and more every year thereafter). If you leave

$100 in the bank and don't withdraw any of the $100 principal or the accumulated interest, at 5 percent, your money will *double* in less than fifteen years (without your adding anything) because of the effect of what is called compound interest, interest on interest ($5) plus principal ($100).

So obviously there is something to be said for putting your money in a bank. But think for a minute. Why should a bank pay you to keep your money? Wouldn't you expect to have to pay for that service instead? The reason the bank is willing to pay for interest is that it uses the money you deposit; it puts that money to work. Instead of simply keeping all of the money of all its depositors in a vault, the bank sets aside some money to take care of withdrawals and puts the rest to work to earn more money. It may, for example, lend money to people who seem likely to repay that money at a certain designated time. And since the rate of interest that a borrower of money must pay the bank is higher than the rate of interest that depositors of money receive, the bank makes a profit with your money. The bank may also buy certain kinds of securities with some of its funds, securities such as bonds and stocks. When the bank buys bonds, it is lending money to the government or corporation that issued the bond and receiving interest for the use of that money. When the bank buys stock, it is becoming part owner of the corporation that issued the stock. In short, the bank is using your money to make a profit for itself.

Now there's nothing wrong with that, since you are getting from the bank the safekeeping of your money and interest as well. Your money is there when you need it for an emergency or want it to buy something. But it may occur to you that if your bank can make money with your money — enough money to pay the interest due on what you have deposited and a profit besides — perhaps you can do the same on your own. Perhaps you can buy securities, bonds and stocks, and make more money than you can with a bank account.

Taking Things into Your Own Hands

You can indeed. But there is something you had better take into account before you put your money anywhere, and that is that the greater the possible return, the higher the risk. And, of course, the smaller the potential return, the lower the risk. That's a principle that works in most aspects of life, as a matter of fact (just as the law of supply and demand does). The man who goes out prospecting for gold hasn't much chance of finding it because it's hard to find — but if he does find it, he may be rich overnight. He has taken a big risk and found a great reward — but he might easily have lost. In fact, he is more likely to lose than to gain. It is also true that a man who looks for something that is relatively easy to find is more likely to find it — and less likely to be well rewarded for his trouble. The whole question of risk and reward is a big one that we'll have more to say about later.

Keep in mind that there are just three things you can do with money. You can save it or lend it or spend it. Obviously, you must spend some to live. You can put your money in the bank where it will earn interest for you and be there when you want it. But don't forget the possible loss of purchasing power if you put your money in the bank. You can lend it by buying bonds or spend it buying stocks — if you're willing to take some additional risks.

There's nothing you can do about the purchasing power of dollars you must spend today. For that matter, there's not

14

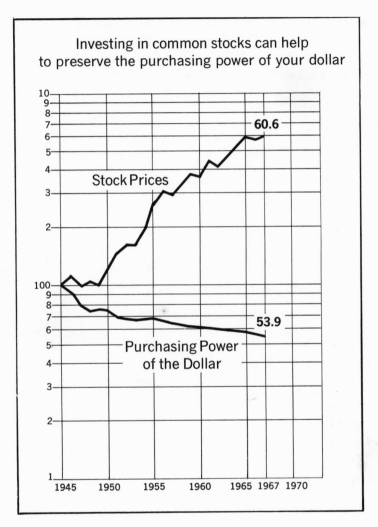

Investing in common stocks can help
to preserve the purchasing power of your dollar

Stock Prices

60.6

Purchasing Power
of the Dollar

53.9

much that you as an individual can do about declining purchasing power at all. What you can do is postpone some of your wants (but not your needs) and invest in the hope of having *more* dollars in the future.

3.

Who Owns Securities and Why?

As we said in the last chapter, it may occur to you that you can put your money to work yourself instead of turning it over to a bank which will do so for itself. Not only *can* you; more than 24,000,000 Americans do just that. One American in ten has put his money to work by buying stock.

Who are those 24,000,000 Americans? Well, about half are men and half are women. (About 1,300,000 are children — 55 percent boys, 45 percent girls — but they can't own stock solely in their own names until they are twenty-one years old. Before that, an adult has to be the custodian of the stock.) The largest age group is forty-five to fifty-four years. About one-third of all stockholders are college graduates. About one-third are housewives. Many other stockholders are people in professional and technical fields, in clerical and sales work, and managers or proprietors of businesses.

The North Central part of the country has the largest number of stockholders, followed by the Middle Atlantic states, with the Pacific Coast area coming up fast. California has the largest number of stockholders of any one state — more than 2,500,000. (It also has the largest population, of course.)

Capitalists Come in All Sizes

And here's an eye-opening fact. You might guess that most stockholders would be wealthy people, people with large sums of money to spare after paying their daily living expenses. That's the way things used to be. But now one-third of all stockholders have annual incomes under $7,500 and more than half earn less than $10,000. In other words, there are capitalists in all income brackets and all walks of life.

There are stockholders in other free-enterprise countries, too, but no one is sure of the exact number. Japan is probably second after the United States, followed by Britain, France, Italy, and West Germany.

Once before in our country's history there were a great many people who owned stocks. That was in the 1920's. But things were different then. Many people went into debt to buy stock instead of buying only what they could pay for with accumulated savings. When stock prices fell in 1929, they lost everything they had. There were also crooks who took advan-

18

tage of unwary stockholders in a variety of ways and caused them to lose money.

Things are very much different today. In 1933 and 1934 and again in 1940 and 1965, Congress passed laws regulating the securities business and putting an end to most of the practices by which stockholders had been fleeced. Congress also established a government agency called the Securities and Exchange Commission. That commission, usually called by its initials, SEC, consists of five men appointed by the President with the advice and consent of the Senate. They serve five-year terms which rotate so that there is one new commissioner every year. No more than three of the commissioners can be from one political party. The SEC keeps an eye on the securities business and enforces the law in a variety of ways. We'll have more to say later about the SEC and about the securities laws of the various states, which are known as blue-sky laws.

But we've strayed from our subject — the number of stockholders in the United States. More than 24,000,000 Americans have taken money that they might have used to buy a new car or an oil painting or a summer cottage and have chosen to buy stock instead. Why?

The Lure of Investing

Quite simply, to make money. They saw banks making money by putting money to work, and they decided to try to do it for themselves. They also decided that instead of enjoying spending their money now, they would rather put it to work, try to make it increase, and enjoy spending more of it *later*.

Does that mean that buying stocks is an infallible way to make money — a way that can't miss? No indeed. As with everything else in life, there is an element of risk — just as there is

19

an element of risk in crossing a street or even in taking a bath. You can, of course, avoid the risk of losing money by *not* buying stocks. But remember what happens to money that is put in a cookie jar or even a savings account: its purchasing power gets smaller and smaller. That's why people buy stocks.

Now there are stocks and stocks, some good for some purposes, others good for other purposes, still others good for no purpose at all — good for nothing. For many years, it was generally believed that when you bought stocks, you were more likely to make money than to lose it, but there was no proof. Then the University of Chicago set up a Center for Research in Security Prices (sometimes called CRISP), and, using a computer to make the more than 52,000,000 calculations necessary, determined that in the thirty-five years from 1926 through 1960, stockholders made profits 78 percent of the time, and their profits averaged 9 percent each year compounded annually before taxes. To put it another way, that means that more than three stock purchases out of every four were profitable. And thanks to compounding (interest on interest plus principal), the average dollar invested and returning 9 percent increased to $20 in thirty-five years. Is it any wonder that more than 24,000,000 Americans own stock?

4.

Business: Its Reasons for Being

Ours is an economy based on business. Or, as President Calvin Coolidge put it, "The business of America is business." The famous American standard of living, the highest in the world, would be much lower if it were not for American business, which produced an estimated $785,000,000,000 worth of goods and services in 1967 — more than in any previous year and probably less than in future years.

21

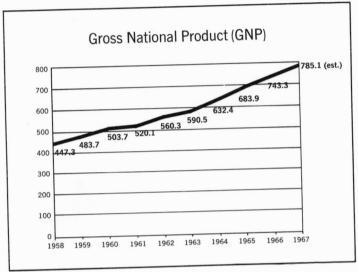

Gross National Product (GNP)

COURTESY OF MERRILL LYNCH, PIERCE, FENNER & SMITH INC.

Why Business?

Business corporations exist for several reasons. If they are successful, they make money for their owners, they give employment to workers, and they provide the public with goods and services that are needed and wanted. But they cannot do any of these things unless they have money to begin and to grow. Raw materials and factories and offices obviously cost money — a great deal of money. American business corporations will probably spend about $65,000,000,000 for new plants and equipment in 1968, and that figure doesn't take into account at all the value of all the plants and equipment now in use.

Why such an enormous sum of money? Because a worker without a place to work and tools to work with can't do much. It costs somewhere around $25,000 to $30,000 to provide the equipment for *one* worker, and there are some 76,000,000 workers in the United States. Without the money, there wouldn't be jobs. That's why we said earlier that money is the lifeblood of the nation. The question is, where does that money come from?

John Jackson, Entrepreneur*

Let's consider the case of John Jackson, the son of a widow who is famous in her town for her delicious breads and cakes and cookies. With money somewhat scarce in the Jackson household, John and his mother decide to sell some of Mrs. Jackson's baked goods from door to door. So Mrs. Jackson bakes all day, and John sells what she makes before and after school. The business is such a success that when John finishes his schooling, he decides to open a shop and sell his mother's baked goods there.

But right away he needs money. His mother can't do all the baking in her own kitchen, so he has to equip a kitchen and hire people to help with the baking and selling and set up a shop in a good location. All those things cost money. But he must do them if he wants his business to succeed and grow. Where is that money going to come from?

The Jacksons have some money saved, but they have to spend most of their income on day-to-day living expenses, so they haven't enough for the raw materals and the kitchen equipment and the rent for the store and the display cases and

* French for "enterpriser" or businessman.

23

boxes and cash register and all the rest. Then where can John Jackson turn? He might try to get a loan from his bank and pay it back out of the proceeds from the shop. But suppose the bank thinks he has too little business experience to make a go of the shop and refuses to give him the loan? He might also borrow from friends, but John is too proud to do that, and he doesn't want his friends telling him how to run his business as they might if they put money into it.

Here's another possibility. He might consider taking in a partner, someone who will put money into the business and work there, too. John had a classmate at school who might be interested — and he is. Dick Richards agrees to join the bakery enterprise — to put in money that he has saved and to share the work and the profits or losses. John and Dick each put in $5,000 and agree to share everything on a 60 percent–40 percent basis — in recognition of the fact that John started the business and has more know-how than Dick. The money enables them to make down payments on the equipment they need. The people who sell them the ovens and refrigerator and cash register in effect lend money to John and Dick by extending credit to them, by letting them have the equipment they need and finish paying for it over a period of time. It costs more money to buy equipment that way than to pay for it all at once, but they have no choice.

So the Jackson Bakery opens, and it succeeds because the baked goods are delicious and the shop is conveniently located for its customers and the prices are low enough to attract customers and high enough to enable the partners to make a profit, even after paying off the cost of their equipment. Naturally, before long the partners decide that if they can succeed with one shop, they can increase their profits by opening other shops.

Money-Hunting

And what is the first problem they have to face? Money again. Expansion means more raw materials and more equipment and more employees. It means more money than the partners have in spite of the success of the bakery. They can, of course, go to the bank, which may be more willing to lend money now that they have a going concern. Or they can take in more partners. But they decide to take another course.

First of all, they incorporate their business. They turn their partnership into a corporation by having their lawyer file the necessary papers and pay the necessary fees to the state. The corporation can buy or sell property and can sue or be sued. The owners of the corporation (John and Dick, in this instance) are not *personally* responsible for the debts of the corporation. That is, their personal property cannot be appropriated by the people to whom the corporation owes money if they fail to pay, while the personal property of the partners in a partnership can. The British call the same kind of company a limited liability company — to indicate that the owners can lose only as much as they own of the company and no more.

Having incorporated, John and Dick have another way to obtain the money they need to expand the Jackson Bakery Corporation. They can sell securities in their corporation to the public; then they are said to "go public." And what are securities? Stocks and bonds. Stocks are shares in the ownership of a corporation, and bonds are a way for a corporation to borrow money. John and Dick decide that selling securities is the answer for them. But which kind of securities? If they sell *bonds,* they will have to repay the amount of the bonds eventually and in the meantime they will have to pay interest to the people who buy the bonds. On the other hand, bondholders have nothing to say about the way a company is run, generally speaking. And there is a tax advantage to the corporation in selling bonds instead of stocks: A corporation does not have to pay taxes on the interest that it pays to its bondholders.

If John and Dick decide to sell *stock,* they don't have to repay the amount of the stock or pay any interest at all, since the people who buy stock are owners, not lenders. But John and Dick will no longer be sole owners of the corporation. They will continue to run the business, but they will have to submit some major decisions to the stockholders for approval. And they will be expected to share any future profits with the stockholders in the form of dividends — on which the corporation must pay taxes (unlike bond interest) before sending the dividends to their stockholders. In short, there are advantages and disadvantages to the company both ways.

Going Public

John and Dick talk over their problem with their lawyer, who tells them that a small corporation is likely to have a hard time selling bonds and recommends that they raise the money they need for expansion by selling stock instead. They agree that they would rather sell shares in the business than have the corporation go into debt so early in its life. Their lawyer puts them in touch with an investment banker who will underwrite the stock — that is, buy it from the corporation and sell it to the public for a fee or profit. The fee will be based on the number of shares to be sold, the price of the shares, and the investment banker's opinion of how difficult it will be to sell the shares. Since the corporation is small and is known only in its own locality, the chances are that local investors will be the buyers of the stock.

And so the stock of the Jackson Bakery Corporation is sold to the public, and John and Dick get a check from the investment banker for the proceeds. From then on, the price of the stock is never set again. It goes up and down in accordance with the law of supply and demand among investors. The company may own little or none of its own stock and therefore generally does not make or lose money as its stock moves up and down in price.

The bakery expands. If it prospers, it may become a big corporation with a large bakery and a chain of stores, and in time the corporation may sell more stock or issue bonds to raise funds for further expansion. Or it may find itself losing money and be forced to go out of business, as happens to many small businesses every year (more than twelve thousand in 1967). But John and Dick have a good start, and there is every reason to believe that the Jackson Bakery Corporation is on its way to bigger things.

5.

Bonds: What They Are, Who Buys Them, and Why

We're getting a bit ahead of ourselves. It's time we defined some more terms and talked more about what stocks are and what bonds are and how they differ. *Securities* is a blanket word for both stocks and bonds, but that's one of the few things thay have in common, even though they are both ways of putting your money to work.

Borrowers and Lenders

Let's consider bonds first. A bond is essentially an IOU given by a government or a corporation to a person or organization that lends money to it. It is a promise to repay a certain sum of money on a certain date and to pay a certain rate of interest in the meantime. The government or corporation is called the issuer, and the person or organization lending the money is a bondholder or creditor. Issuers usually borrow money in units of $1,000, which means that bonds are issued in units of $1,000 and are said to have a face value of $1,000. That means that the issuer guarantees to pay the bondholder $1,000 at the end of a certain stated period of time and to pay interest at a certain rate until then for the use of the money. All that information — the face value, the interest rate, and the date due (called the maturity date) — appears on the face of an engraved piece of paper called a certificate. If you buy a corporation's bond, you get the company's IOU plus interest until you cash in the bond at maturity.

Bonds come in two forms, bearer and registered. If you buy a *bearer bond,* you get a piece of paper with a lot of coupons attached, and each coupon has a date and an amount of interest engraved on it. Whenever the date shown on a coupon comes around — usually every six months — you clip the coupon and present it to your bank. Your bank undertakes to collect the interest from the issuer and either gives you the money or credits it to your account. The reason this kind of bond is called a bearer bond is that it does not show the name of the owner. The bearer, the person who holds the bond or the cou-

Debenture of Xerox Corporation with coupons attached. PETER STEINER PHOTO, COURTESY OF XEROX CORPORATION.

pon, is presumed to be the owner. That means that anyone can redeem the bond or collect the interest, so if you own such a bond, you had better keep it in a safe place (a safe-deposit box in a bank, for example), because if you lose it, it's finders keepers.

Actually, bearer bonds are being issued less and less frequently. Most new bonds are *registered bonds,* which means that the name of the owner of the bond is registered with the issuer, and the issuer sends the bondholder a check for the appropriate amount of interest whenever that interest comes due. There are no coupons on a registered bond.

IOU $25. *Signed:* Uncle Sam

There are many different kinds of bonds, the most common being government bonds, municipal bonds, and corporate bonds. You are probably familiar with one kind of United States Government bond, the Series E savings bond. Series E savings bonds come in denominations (that is, with face values) of $25, $50, $75, $100, $200, $500, $1,000, and $10,000 and pay interest at the rate of 4.25 percent if held seven years and nine months to maturity. This most familiar kind of bond is not typical, however. Uncle Sam does not send you a check for the interest due, even though your name is recorded as the owner. Nor are there coupons to clip. Instead, you buy the bond at a discount, paying less than the face value, and you collect both the interest and the face value in one lump sum when the bond matures. For example, you pay $18.75 for a Series E savings bond, and you can cash it in seven years and nine months later for $25. If you cash it in before the maturity date, you'll get less than $25, but you'll always get at least as much as you paid, $18.75, plus any interest due.

31

There are other kinds of U. S. Government bonds, too. (In fact, the governments of virtually all capitalistic countries borrow money from their citizens by issuing bonds, but we are concerned here only with the United States Government.) Every week the United States Government issues Treasury Bills. They are issued at a discount (like savings bonds), mature in ninety-one days, and are then redeemed at face value — $1,000 or some multiple of $1,000. They do not pay interest; the income from Treasury Bills is the difference between your purchase price and the sale price or maturity value. Thus you might buy a Treasury Bill for $980.67, hold it for ninety-one days, and cash it in for $1,000. Your profit would be the difference between your $980.67 purchase price and the $1,000 maturity value — $19.33. On a percentage basis, that's 5.24 percent per year return on your money.

Except for savings bonds and Treasury Bills, all United States Government bonds are issued at face value, which is also called par value. There are Certificates of Indebtedness, which mature in a year or less and have a fixed rate of interest, which is paid when the Certificate is redeemed. There are Treasury Notes, which run from one to five years and pay interest twice a year. And there are Treasury Bonds, which usually run for five to fifteen years or more and pay various interest rates. Several agencies of the federal government also issue bonds to finance their activities.

An individual who wants to buy Treasury Bonds may do so, but in practice most Treasury Bonds are bought by large organizations such as banks, insurance companies, pension plans, labor unions, and universities.

Why does the United States Government issue bonds — that is, borrow money? To finance its multitude of enterprises while waiting for tax money and other kinds of income to come in. It issues short-term bonds to raise money that it needs for only a short time and longer-term bonds for money needed for a longer time.

And why do investors buy United States Government bonds? For several reasons. One is that they know their money is absolutely safe — as safe as the government itself, which stands behind the bonds. So the buyers of the bonds know that they can count on getting the face value of their bonds back at maturity and the interest in the meantime. Another reason is that United States Government bonds can be turned into cash very quickly if cash is needed. (Such bonds are said to be liquid.) The holders do not have to hold their bonds until maturity; they can sell them any time to a dealer in United States Government bonds. A third reason is that United States Government bonds pay interest (the rate varies, of course), while cash that is kept in a strongbox does not.

Communities Borrow, Too

States and cities also find themselves in the same predicament as the federal government: They need money for new facilities and have to borrow to pay for them. Like the federal government, state and local governments borrow by issuing bonds which are sold to the public. Those bonds are called municipal bonds, and this is the way they come into existence:

Suppose the town in which you live needs a new high school. If the town sets aside part of the cost of a new high school every year out of taxes, it may have enough in thirty years or so. But the town can't wait thirty years for the new school, and neither can the architect and builders be expected to wait thirty years to be paid.

So what happens? The officials of your town submit a proposal to raise funds for a new high school by means of a bond issue to residents of the town at an election. If the bond issue is approved by the voters (the general public), the town then offers its school bonds for sale to the public through a financial firm — just as John Jackson and Dick Richards offered shares of stock in the Jackson Bakery Corporation to the public through a financial firm, an investment banker. The proceeds from the sale of the bonds to the public are used to pay for the new school. The bonds are issued serially — that is, so that a certain number come due each year for, say, from one to twenty-five years, with a slightly different interest rate for each year. Generally speaking, the later the bonds mature, the higher the rate of interest they pay in the meantime. By issuing serial bonds, the community can pay off its debt on the installment plan, retiring a certain number of bonds every year and repaying the face value and paying the interest due out of tax money.

Freedom from Taxes

Who buys municipal bonds? Who lends communities the money to pay for such improvements as schools, hospitals, streets and highways, bridges and tunnels, power plants, waterworks, sewage systems, and such? The answer is institutions (especially commercial banks) and, among individual investors, wealthy people, and the reasons are two. One is that municipal bonds are regarded as very safe investments — almost as safe as United States Government bonds. The record shows that very few communities have ever defaulted — that is, failed to pay back their bonds and to pay the stated interest on them. The second reason that wealthy people buy municipal bonds is that interest on them is exempt (free) from federal income tax — and often from state income tax as well. The federal government, recognizing the importance to states and cities of being able to raise funds to build and maintain needed facilities, helps to make the bonds more attractive to institutions and wealthy people by making the income on them tax exempt. Anybody can buy a municipal bond; they are not restricted to institutions and wealthy people. But among individual investors, wealthy people, people who pay a relatively large proportion of their income in taxes, are the people most interested in the tax-free income that municipal bonds provide.

For example, a married man with an annual income of $50,000 has to pay federal income tax at a rate of 50 percent. If he buys municipal bonds that pay an income in the form of interest of $3\frac{1}{2}$ percent a year, he doesn't have to pay tax on that $3\frac{1}{2}$ percent. If he invests his money in some other way, he has to get at least 7 percent taxable return if he wants to keep half or $3\frac{1}{2}$ percent of it — and 7 percent interest is pretty hard to find.

Corporations Get into the Act

Another important kind of bond is a corporate bond, a bond issued by a corporation. A corporate bond is essentially the same as a government bond or a municipal bond: It is a way for a corporation to borrow money to pay for plant and equipment, for expansion and development. The corporation issuing the bond (through an investment banker) pays interest for the use of the money and repays the face value at maturity, and the bondholders who lend money to the corporation by buying its bonds collect interest as long as they hold the bonds.

When people borrow money — from a bank, for instance — they generally have to put up something as a guarantee that they will pay back what they borrow. The word for what they put up is *collateral*. Collateral may be anything of recognized value — securities, real estate, valuable jewels, etc. Or sometimes the bank may lend money just because the person borrowing has a steady job and hence a regular income and because he has a reputation for always paying his bills on time (a good credit rating).

Corporations borrowing money by issuing bonds are in somewhat the same situation. Before people will lend their money by buying bonds, they want some kind of assurance of repayment. Federal and local governments borrow money mostly on reputation and taxing power. Corporations may offer any of several kinds of collateral when they borrow money by issuing bonds. Some large, well-known corporations such as American Telephone and Telegraph, General Motors, General Electric, and Standard Oil of New Jersey offer only their reputation and issue a kind of bond called a debenture. Others pledge their property — their plant and equipment — and issue mortgage bonds. Still others pledge the securities of other corporations and issue collateral trust bonds. And this list doesn't include all kinds of bonds by any means. The point is that a bond is generally backed by something of value, either reputation or property that can be sold to pay off the bonds if necessary. Some corporations even establish what is called a sinking fund, which is a fund into which they pay money periodically in order to have enough to pay off their bonds when they come due.

If you want to buy a bond, you don't necessarily have to buy it when it is first issued, and you don't have to hold it to maturity, either. Most bonds can be bought or sold any time during their life. But the only time you can be sure of getting the full face value (usually $1,000) if you sell is on the maturity date. Before that, the price of the bond may be either more or less than its face value. If it is selling for less than its face value, the bond is said to be selling at a discount. If it is selling for more than its face value, it is said to be selling at a premium. Even though the price of the bond may fluctuate, the interest is always paid on the face value, so you always know exactly how much interest you are going to get.

Here's something else to remember about bonds. The return is likely to be in proportion to the risk. That means that a bond that pays a very high rate of interest probably isn't quite so safe — so sure to make all its interest payments on time and to pay the full face value at maturity — as a bond that pays a lower rate of interest. Risk may depend on many things, particularly time (because the distant future is less predictable than the near future) and the reputation of the issuer (based on past experience). In other words, as we've said before, you have to be willing to take a higher risk for a higher return — or to be content with a lower return and have a smaller risk.

There are a few other facts about bonds that you should know. One is that some bonds have call provisions — or, to put it another way, that they are callable. That means simply that the issuer of the bond reserves the right to call in the bond before its date of maturity. That means that you might have to cash in your bond before you expected to do so. And of course the interest would stop as soon as the bond was redeemed. If a bond is callable, the certificate will say so and give the date after which it is callable and the price, which may be the face value or perhaps a bit more, a premium.

No person or institution could possibly know all there is to know about the issuers of municipal and corporate bonds, because there are thousands of issues on the market. Fortunately for investors, there are two independent financial-research services which collect information on most of the larger issues and rate the bonds, taking into account the risks involved and sizing up the relative attractiveness of the issues in the light of the available information. The ratings, starting with the best and going down, go like this — somewhat like school marks:

Moody's	Aaa	Aa	A	Baa	Ba	B	Caa	Ca	C
Standard & Poor's	AAA	AA	A	BBB	BB	B	CCC	CC	C

Bonds Come First

Bonds are sometimes called senior securities, not because they are older than other securities but for two other reasons. One is that bond interest must be paid to the owners by the issuer before the issuer pays out money for dividends on the company's stock. The other is that if the issuer goes broke, the bondholders have first claim on whatever the issuer owns. Thus if a corporation goes out of business, it may sell its plant and equipment, and the people who own the corporation's bonds are then entitled to a share of the money realized from the sale before the owners (stockholders) get any money at all.

A bond, then, is an IOU or a promissory note. It is a way for an organization to borrow money, for which it pays interest, and a way for a person or an institution to lend money, for which he or it receives interest — usually over a fairly long period of time. Bonds are generally regarded as the safest kind of security because interest payments are fixed and predictable, because bond prices are relatively stable (that is, they don't go up and down very much), and because the owner of a bond is pretty sure to get his money back when the bond matures.

6.

Stocks: Common and Preferred, and the Difference Between Them

We have already talked a little bit about stocks, but there's a lot more to say about them. The first and most important thing to remember about stock is that it represents part ownership of a corporation. If the corporation has 10,000 shares of stock outstanding and you own 100 of them, you own $\frac{1}{100}$ of the company. And what does your part ownership of stock entitle you to?

Owning a Company

First of all, ownership of stock means ownership interest in everything that belongs to the corporation — its plant, its raw materials, its inventory, its capital, its profits. That doesn't, of course, mean that you can march up to your company and walk off with $\frac{1}{100}$ of anything — but you wouldn't want to do that anyway. After all, you want the company to prosper. That's why you bought the stock in the first place.

There are two basic kinds of stock, *preferred stock* and *common stock*. Both represent ownership, and the holders of both kinds of stock are entitled to receive regular reports on their company's financial condition. But there the similarity ends.

Generally speaking, owners of common stock may vote for the directors of their company who in turn choose the officers who run the company, while the holders of preferred stock usually have no vote. If a company prospers and pays a return to its stockholders in the form of a dividend, the owners of the common stock may receive a greater return in a good year and a smaller one in a bad year, while the owners of the preferred stock receive a fixed amount each year. The price per share of common stock is likely to move up and down with the company's fortunes, while the price of the preferred stock remains fairly steady.

Is Preferred Preferred?

You may well wonder why common stock is called common and preferred is called preferred, since it appears that many of the advantages are with the common. The answer is that the owners of the preferred stock come first. They get preferential treatment from the company in two ways. One is that if the corporation that issued the stock goes out of business and its property is sold, the holders of the preferred stock are entitled to a share of the proceeds before the holders of the common stock get anything at all. (But remember that the corporation's bondholders, if there are any, have rights that come before even the rights of the holders of the preferred stock.) The holders of the preferred are also entitled to receive their dividends — usually a specified amount — before the holders of the common stock receive any dividends at all (but after the interest due the bondholders has been paid). That means that in a lean year when the company doesn't make much money, first the bond interest will be paid and then the dividends on the preferred stock — and the owners of the common stock may receive little or nothing. In other words, if there isn't enough to go around, the holders of the common stock are the ones who do without their dividends.

Some preferred stocks are called *cumulative preferred,* and that means simply that if the company has to skip the dividend on its preferred stock for a year or two, it has to pay any back dividends plus the dividend due currently to the preferred stockholders before it can pay anything at all to the owners of the common stock. But the owners of the preferred stock never receive more than a set amount, even if the company has a banner year. Dividends are, of course, the income that stockholders receive on their investment, usually quarterly payments of cash or sometimes additional stock.

Dividend ÷ Price = Yield

Incidentally, when people talk about dividends, they may talk in terms of dollars. But if they want to compare what one

41

company pays with what another pays, a better way to do it is to compare yields, which are percentages of the value of the stock instead of dollar amounts. The reason is that it doesn't make sense to compare dividends alone. If you paid $25 for a share of stock that pays $2 in dividends, you are obviously getting a better return than if you paid $50 for a share of stock and get $2 in dividends. You need to compare both the amount of the dividends and the price of the stock, and to do that, you compare what is called yield. To get the yield, you take the dividend and divide it by the price of the stock. In the first instance, $2 divided by $25 is 8 percent — a very high yield. In the second instance, $2 divided by $50 is 4 percent, which is just about average. You can see how much easier it is to compare yields than prices-plus-dividends.

Now if you had your choice between owning shares of the preferred stock of a good company — shares that would change very little in value and pay about 5 percent regularly every year — and owning shares of the common stock — shares that might increase or decrease considerably in value and might or might not pay a dividend — which would you choose? Most people would choose common stock. That is, most people *have* chosen common stock. Why? Because they believe the rewards of common stock outweigh the risks. Because they are willing to take the chance of losing some money in exchange for the chance of gaining some money. (And remember that the University of Chicago says they're right; they're likely to make money three times out of four.)

Those people could, of course, have chosen to buy bonds which would pay regular fixed interest and the full face value at maturity — which would keep their money quite safe and pay a regular return. Or they could perhaps get a slightly higher rate of return on preferred stocks with no guarantee of getting the face value back but very little likelihood of losing their money. But they paid their money and they took their choice, and most investors chose common stock.

The reasons aren't hard to find. There is excitement as well as the possibility of profit in buying a stock and watching its price move up and down. And there is always the possibility that if the company has a very profitable year, the directors will vote to increase the dividend on the common stock.

Do They or Don't They?

A few words about dividends may be in order. First of all, no company is obliged to pay any dividends on its common stock — and in fact some companies don't pay dividends at all. It is up to the directors of the company to decide whether the company should pay dividends, and their decision is likely to be based in part on the amount of the company's profits (usually called earnings), since dividends are generally paid out of earnings. In general, if a company pays a certain dividend at the end of one quarter of the year, it is expected to pay a dividend of at least as much in the next quarter. And if the dividend is passed — that is, if the directors decide to omit it — the price of the stock is likely to drop because investors may think it is a less profitable investment than it was. In other words, a company that pays a dividend is expected to continue to pay a dividend of at least as much every quarter. How much of a company's profits are likely to be paid out in dividends? There is no rule, but during 1966 the pay-out ratio, the proportion of profits paid out in dividends, averaged 46 percent of earnings for 844 widely held companies.

But what about companies that pay no dividends at all? Does anybody buy their stock? Yes indeed. Instead of paying dividends to their stockholders, some companies put their profits right back into the company, using the money to build a new plant or buy new machinery or develop a new product or benefit the company in some way. Companies that are in such highly competitive and fast-growing industries as office equipment and electronics and drugs are likely to use most of their earnings for expansion and improvements. (For example, for years IBM stock yielded 1 percent or less; yet it is one of the most widely held stocks in the United States.) And investors, far from avoiding the stocks of such companies, may take the view that in the long run such stocks may be worth more than the stocks that pay out part of their earnings to their stockholders.

A Hybrid in the Stock Market

There's another security that's a kind of hybrid. It's a corporate bond or preferred stock that can be exchanged for the common stock of the same company, and it's called a convertible. It works this way. Let's say you buy a company's bond for $1,000 and it is convertible into 20 shares of the company's common stock. As long as the price of the common stock is $50 or less, you will hold the bond and not convert it into stock because anything under $50 × 20 shares is less than $1,000, and you would not only get less than the value of the bond but you would also give up the relative stability of the bond for the ups and downs of the stock. But if the stock were to go over $50 a share and if it seemed likely to stay there, you would probably convert from the bond into the stock. With a convertible, the choice is yours, so you hold whichever security seems likely to be more profitable for you. Just remember that once you have converted to stock, you can't convert back to bonds again — unless you sell your stock and start all over again. A convertible isn't convertible both ways.

Why the Ups and Downs?

What makes stock prices go up and down? If we knew the answer to that question, we could make a great deal of money by buying low and selling high. But nobody does know the answer, perhaps because there are actually many answers. The price of a stock may go up and down with the fortunes of the company, of course. But it may also fluctuate seemingly for no reason at all or for a reason that seems to have nothing to do with the company directly. For example, stock prices fell when President Kennedy was assassinated, even though that tragic event had no direct bearing on the fortunes of most companies.

The answer to the question, "What makes stock prices move up and down?" is, "Nobody knows." Prices fluctuate because people's opinions of company prospects fluctuate for any of a thousand reasons. Price fluctuations reflect human behavior, which is never wholly predictable. That's one reason so many people find the stock market fascinating.

7.

Over the Counter: What Does It Mean?

How is it that stock prices go up and down anyway? And why should they? If you buy 50 shares of stock in the Jackson Bakery Corporation, aren't those shares worth what you paid for them?

Well, yes and no. That, by the way, is a typical Wall Street answer. There always seem to be things to say on two — or more — sides of any question. A stock always has what is called a *book value*, which is the value behind each share, based on the company's balance sheet of assets and liabilities. To find the book value of Jackson Bakery stock, for example, you would add up the value of all the company's tangible assets (kitchen equipment, inventory of raw materials, cash registers and showcases, delivery trucks, and such), and divide by the number of shares of common stock outstanding. What you paid for your shares of Jackson Bakery stock may or may not be close to the book value of the stock.

Why Are Prices So Changeable?

But the value of a share of stock is not a fixed amount that changes only when assets and liabilities change. Its true value is not even what you paid for it but *what you can sell it for.*

There is an old saying: A thing is worth what it will fetch. A share of stock is worth what it will fetch. And that is a figure that is constantly changing as people's opinions change regarding the company and its chance of making a profit and the size of the profit. It's the law of supply and demand at work again. If many people think that the Jackson Bakery will make a substantial profit and if they decide to buy the stock, the price will probably go up because the demand is greater than the supply. And the situation may be reversed, too, of course.

But how can the price go up and down? Isn't the price of Jackson Bakery stock set just the way the price of one of the bakery's layer cakes is set? The answer is *no*. The price of a stock is set when that stock is first issued — and never again. When John Jackson and Dick Richards decided to raise money to expand the Jackson Bakery by issuing stock and selling it to the public, the price was set, based on book value at that time.

But from that time on, the price of the stock is always a compromise between what buyers are willing to pay and what owners are willing to sell for.

And how do you know what that amount is? Can you walk into Jackson Bakery and ask? Will they sell you ten shares of stock along with a cherry pie and a half-dozen doughnuts? No. You have to buy the stock from someone who already owns it, from a Jackson Bakery stockholder. That's because the company issued only a limited number of shares to get the money it needed at the time. So the only way to buy a share now is to buy it from somebody who already owns it.

And how do you go about finding a Jackson Bakery stockholder? Well, you can ask all your friends. You can put an ad in your local newspaper. You can pick up the telephone and start calling people. But the chances of your finding a Jackson Bakery stockholder who wants to sell aren't very good. You need help.

Help!

That's where a broker comes in. A stockbroker is a man representing a company that is in the business of buying and selling stocks for people like you who want to put their money to work to make more money. A stockbroker can find a Jackson Bakery stockholder who wants to sell some stock; that is his business. And for finding that stockholder and buying the stock for you, he will charge you an amount of money — usually between 1 percent and 5 percent of the total cost of the stock — for his service.

How does he know where to find a seller? The simple answer is that he makes it his business to know. But to explain further, he is in touch by telephone with other brokers not only in the town but all over the country. And he subscribes to a service (not available to the general public) called "the daily pink sheets," which contain lists of stocks and the brokers prepared to buy or sell them and the prices at which they bought and sold them on the preceding business day. So by referring to the pink sheets and telephoning brokers whose names appear opposite the name of Jackson Bakery, your broker can find a seller for you.

What Does That Funny Name Mean?

What we are describing is the so-called over-the-counter market, which is a vast national market without a central marketplace — a market in which buyers and sellers and brokers may never meet but do business by teletype and telephone, bargaining with one another over prices, which change all the time. The name *over the counter* is confusing. Some people think it means they can buy stocks over the counter or off the shelf as they would buy merchandise in a store. And that's just how it was in the early days of our country's history. It is no longer true, but the old name has stuck over the years, despite many suggestions to change it.

Now suppose you want to buy some shares of Jackson Bakery stock. You walk into a broker's office in your town. Perhaps the broker's name was given to you by a friend. Perhaps you just found the name in the yellow pages. It doesn't matter because you don't need an introduction or permission — as long as you are at least twenty-one years old. Just be sure that your broker is reputable by asking a banker or lawyer or Better Business Bureau or Chamber of Commerce.

If all you want is information, he will probably be glad to provide it. But if you want to do business — buy or sell some

49

A busy over-the-counter department in a brokerage firm, where traders negotiate purchases and sales by telephone with other traders.
PHOTO COURTESY OF MERRILL LYNCH, PIERCE, FENNER & SMITH INC.

securities — you have to open an account. That's a fairly simple procedure, very much like opening a charge account in a department store. You fill out a form giving your name, address, telephone, Social Security number, occupation and place of business, age (remember you must be over twenty-one), and a credit reference such as a bank. The credit reference is necessary because generally a broker transacts your business and then sends you a bill, and he has to be sure that you have the means to pay. Or if you are selling, he needs some assurance that you will deliver the stock he sold for you or make it good.

What Will the Stock Cost?

Once your account is open, let's say you tell your broker that you want to buy some shares of Jackson Bakery stock. You may, of course, ask him what he thinks of the company and its prospects; but in this instance, you've pretty well made up your mind to buy before setting foot in his office. So what you really want to know is the price of the stock. He may look it up for you in the pink sheets and tell you it is trading (that is, being bought and sold) in the neighborhood of 11 to 12 (that is, $11 to $12). So you decide that you want to buy 50 shares.

You tell your broker, and he goes to work, calling several of the other brokers listed on the pink sheets to see which one will give him the best price. One may say $11\frac{1}{8}$–$11\frac{3}{4}$; another may say $11\frac{1}{4}$–$11\frac{7}{8}$; a third may say 11–$11\frac{5}{8}$. The two prices that each broker quotes are the bid and the asked, sometimes called the bid and the offered. The bid is the highest price that anyone is willing to pay for the stock at that moment, and the asked or offered is the lowest price at which anyone is willing to sell at that moment. Obviously, the third asked price is the lowest and therefore the best for you, so your broker buys 50 shares for you from the third broker and bills you for 50 times 11⅝ or $581.25 plus a fee or commission of perhaps $12 or so for acting as your agent in the transaction.

When Is a Broker Not a Broker?

Or the whole transaction might have been handled in a slightly different way. Since Jackson Bakery is a local company well known in the town, your broker may own a quantity of shares of the stock and sell you 50 shares from his own inventory. If he does that, he is not acting as a broker or agent but rather as a dealer or principal, and instead of charging you a fee or commission, he will include his profit in the price that he charges you. Then he is said to "make a market" in the stock, which means that he is prepared to buy or sell shares of that stock at any time, and his bid and asked quotations are carried on the pink sheets so that other dealers know that they can buy the stock from him or sell it to him.

NQB and NASD

It should not make any difference to you as a customer if you buy from a broker or a dealer. The total cost should be substantially the same. One reason is competition. The firm with which you do business is not the only firm making a market in Jackson Bakery stock, and if its price is consistently out of line with the prices of other dealers, it will lose business. And those prices are a matter of record in the pink sheets, which are issued daily by the National Quotation Bureau. Overseeing the whole over-the-counter market is the National Association of Securities Dealers, which in turn is responsible to the Securities and Exchange Commission. The NASD sets standards for the forty-five hundred brokers and dealers in the over-the-counter market, recommends the amount of profit that is reasonable on transactions, and disciplines brokers and dealers who violate its rules, by censuring, fining, suspending, or expelling them.

The NASD also supplies daily over-the-counter quotations to newspapers and wire services for publication on the financial pages of newspapers. If you look in your local newspaper, you will probably be able to follow the price fluctuations of your stock from day to day — in addition to reading any financial news about the company. Look under the heading "Over-the-Counter Quotations" and find Jackson Bakery in its alphabetical position, and you will see the current bid and asked quotations (that is, those of the preceding business day) and sometimes the previous bid (the day before the preceding business day) as well.

Spice of Life

A look at the over-the-counter quotations will give you some idea of the kinds of corporations whose stocks are traded over the counter, but it can give you only an inkling of the size of that market, the number of stocks traded there. In fact, no count has ever been made of the number of corporations with their stocks traded in the over-the-counter market. The number is estimated to be anywhere from 50,000 to 100,000 or more. What kinds of companies are they? Every kind — from small local companies such as Jackson Bakery Corporation to some of the largest corporations in the world, including most banks and insurance companies, many utility companies, many Canadian and foreign companies, and industrial corporations of all kinds and sizes. In addition, all United States Government securities, municipal bond shares, and mutual fund shares are traded in the over-the-counter market.

Some examples of well-known companies whose stocks are traded over the counter are American Express, Anheuser-Busch, Conde Nast, Harper & Row, Jantzen, Inc., Eli Lilly & Co., and A. C. Nielsen Company.

8.

Making a Start in Investing

Now let's suppose that you're all ready to invest. You know what stocks and bonds are. You understand the possible risks as well as the possible rewards of investing. You're of age and have money that's yours to use as you please. What do you do now?

Custom Made

If you have lots of money — say $250,000 or more — you may want to turn that money over to someone else and have him manage it for you. That someone else may be a person or a company acting as an investment counselor under the watchful eye of the SEC. Your investment counselor may either give you continuing advice on your investments or he may take over the management of your investments himself, changing them as he sees fit. The investments and the profits or losses are yours, of course. For his services, the investment counselor may charge you a set fee or — more likely — a percentage of the value of your holdings as of a certain date. The percentage might be in the neighborhood of one-half of 1 percent per year, or $1,250 on investments worth $250,000.

Ready Made

You can also buy investment help in the form of investment advisory services — which give advice on how to select securities and how to time purchases or sales. There are many such services available at varying fees. You may find investment advisory service publications in a broker's office or in your local library, or you may see them advertised in the financial pages of some newspapers. Some are good, some are bad, and nobody is right all the time. The difference between an investment counselor and an investment advisory service is that the counselor tailors his advice to your needs, while the service simply sells its opinions.

There's another ready-made kind of investment available to you if you want to delegate your choice of securities to others.

You can buy shares in an investment company. There are two kinds of investment companies: closed-end companies and open-end companies. In principle, they are much the same. An investment company is a company that invests in other companies instead of manufacturing a product or providing a service. The investment company gets its money from many investors, whose funds are pooled and turned over to a group of managers who invest it as they think appropriate, depending on the purpose of the fund. Thus in effect the buyers of the shares of investment companies are actually buying shares in other companies — whatever companies' securities the managers choose to buy. The managers may change the investment company's holdings whenever they see fit, and for their services they are paid a fee based on the total value of the investment company's holdings.

Closed . . .

One kind of investment company is called a *closed-end* investment company because the number of shares is limited by the company's own bylaws. That means that if you want to buy shares in that company, you must buy them from someone who owns them; and if you want to sell, you must sell to someone who wants to buy — just as you would with shares of common stock. In fact, shares in the largest closed-end investment companies are listed and traded on the New York Stock Exchange and can be bought and sold like common stocks at standard commission rates. The value of the shares in a closed-end investment company moves up and down more or less in relation to the value of the shares of the companies that the investment company owns. That value is changing constantly, of course. At the end of 1966, closed-end investment companies owned shares worth $6.6 billion — a substantial amount but far less than the value of shares owned by open-end investment companies, which was in the neighborhood of $35 billion.

. . . and Open

Open-end investment companies, which are usually called mutual funds, are traded in the over-the-counter market. An investor who wants to buy mutual fund shares must buy them from the company, not from another investor. And when he wishes to sell them, he sells them back to the company — which he can do at any time for a small charge or sometimes no charge. Open-end investment companies issue more shares whenever investors want to buy them — hence the term *open end*. The cost of buying mutual fund shares ranges all the way from nothing (for the so-called no-load funds, which have no salesmen who must be paid) to about 9 percent of the value of the investment. And what is the value of a share? Twice each day the current value of all the holdings of each mutual fund is totaled and divided by the number of shares outstanding to get what is called the net asset value, which of course changes as the value of the fund's holdings change. Thus if a mutual fund owned 500 shares of Company A and 1,000 shares of Company B and 1,200 shares of Company C, the current price of each company would be multiplied by the appropriate number of shares and totaled, and the total would be divided by the number of shares in the fund held by investors.

There are over 500 mutual funds in the United States designed for various investment objectives, so the choice is wide. Some funds pay dividends, just as some stocks do. Other funds plow back most of their earnings (dividends on companies whose stock they own and capital gains from profitable sales of stock) for the sake of faster growth. The aims of the fund are always outlined in the prospectus that is given to everyone who is thinking of purchasing shares in the fund and should be read, just as anyone considering investing on his own should find out about the company whose shares he is thinking of buying before he buys them.

Investment companies have grown tremendously in popularity in recent years. At the end of 1967, some 4,000,000 Americans owned mutual fund shares worth approximately $45,000,000,000, and the funds' holdings had grown eightyfold from 1940 to 1966. Why did so many people buy mutual fund shares? Some bought them because they were afraid to put all their eggs in one basket and they decided that mutual funds offer an opportunity to spread even a small investment over a number of industries and companies. Diversification (the spreading of your investments over different industries and companies) is a way of decreasing the risks of investing — but not necessarily a way of increasing profits. Other investors bought mutual fund shares because they wanted professional management and couldn't afford an investment counselor. And undoubtedly still others bought them because they were subjected to some high-pressure salesmanship at a time when they were open to persuasion.

In fact, investment companies do offer professional management, but the average investment company's shares have actually not increased in value any more than the average share of stock, so the managers haven't covered themselves with glory and haven't brought important benefits to the owners of investment company shares. Also there are two sides to the question of diversification. Suppose you had invested your money in three companies, and one of your stocks did badly and the other two did well. Now suppose you had invested all your

money in one company that did well. You would be better off
in the second instance than in the first, but you would have
taken a greater risk. Spreading your money around gives you
more chances of doing well — or of doing badly. Concentrat-
ing it gives you only one chance of doing *very* well — or *very*
badly. You may remember what we said earlier about risk:
The greater the risk, the greater the potential reward. The
smaller the risk, the smaller the potential reward. To sum up,
investment companies serve a useful purpose for conservative
investors, but they are not for the adventurous.

Choosing Is Hard

What's more, it may actually be more difficult to pick an investment company than to pick a manufacturing or service
company in which to invest. The choice is large, and the only
standard of judgment is past performance, which may or may
not be a good measure. If you invest in a manufacturing or
service company, there are many ways — not just one — of
judging that stock as an investment. For example, there is
likely to be a continuity of product and marketing in a corporation, while an investment company's holdings may change
from week to week — indeed, do change as their managers
change their opinions about the company's holdings and take
steps to try to increase the value of the fund's shares. In 1966,
almost one-third of all mutual fund holdings were changed by
their managers. Since mutual funds have to pay commission
costs when they buy and sell securities, just as individual investors do, and those costs come out of the total value of the
fund's holdings, as does the management fee, you can see that a
substantial amount of your money may be spent without your

ever seeing it if you elect to buy a mutual fund. It is for just such reasons that the SEC undertook a comprehensive study of mutual funds and that Congress in 1967 was considering the enactment of legislation to end the worst abuses.

Do It Yourself

Popular as investment companies are, they are not so popular as what might be called do-it-yourself investing. More than 24,000,000 Americans now own stock directly, and the number is growing yearly. Some received their first stocks as gifts. Some bought the stock of the company where they work under a special stock purchase program. And quite a few first got their feet wet in a small way and then went on to larger investments. What are some of those small ways?

The smallest of all is to start as an armchair investor, watching the stock market without investing a penny. If you want to be an armchair investor, you might, for example, start reading the financial news in a good newspaper every day. The news is likely to mean nothing to you at first, but gradually the pieces will begin to fit and you will begin to see relationships and continuity. Soon you will want to pick a few stocks to watch — perhaps the stocks of companies that make consumer products that you know: your family automobile, a familiar food or drug product, a major appliance, something that is used in the family's recreation — photography, television, reading, a favorite sport. If you keep a week-to-week record of the performance of each stock at the same time you are reading the news, you may see how the news affects stock prices — not just news of the company itself and its products and management and earnings but also news of war and peace, of legislation, of politics, of many other things that may affect stock prices, including earnings reports, management changes, and new product announcements.

Sometimes schools include armchair investing in their social studies courses. Sometimes classes collect small contributions from all members and choose a stock and buy one share to give the class a stake in a company. Both are interesting projects, but of course they have time limits dictated by the length of the semester or school year, and those time limits may not give a stock a chance to perform. Anyway, the chances are that interesting as armchair or classroom investing may be, you will find that it is far less interesting than owning stocks and watching them move — just as a race is more interesting to watch if you have a relative or friend participating or if you have made a wager on the outcome. You care more about the result when you are involved.

MIP

You'll probably want to invest in a small way at first, choosing one of the stocks you followed as an armchair investor and buying shares a few at a time as you can afford them. Remember that a minor can't own stocks in his own name, but one of his parents can act as custodian. Actually, you can buy shares of stock by the dollar's worth (like gasoline or apples) instead of by the share if you buy them through a Monthly Investment Plan account. The Monthly Investment Plan is a way of buying shares of stock in companies listed on the New York Stock Exchange through brokers who are members of the Exchange by depositing as much money as you can afford ($40 minimum) monthly or quarterly or whenever you can. When you buy stocks that way, you have all the privileges of ownership, including the right to vote for directors and the right to your share of any dividends your company pays. Your broker holds your stock and collects your dividends for you and, if you wish, reinvests them automatically in the same stock for you, thus making your investment grow faster than it would otherwise. (Remember the principle of compounding.) You can skip payments or close your MIP account any time without paying any penalty. The cost of buying stocks through the Monthly Investment Plan is the standard New York Stock Exchange commission charge, which your broker deducts from your payments, investing the rest for you. (Since commission charges on small amounts of money are proportionately greater than on larger amounts of money, many MIP investors prefer to make relatively large payments quarterly instead of relatively small payments monthly. Thus if you had $40 a month to invest, you might be better off investing $120 every three months than $40 every month.) All you have to do is open an MIP account, choose your stock, and make payments to your broker. And if you want to buy more than one stock, you simply open more than one MIP account, one for each stock.

An Investing Technique

The Monthly Investment Plan has what might be called an extra added attraction. It enables you to use a technique that is used with considerable success by such institutions as banks, insurance companies, and investment companies — a technique called *dollar cost averaging*. When you dollar cost average, you buy a certain dollar amount of a stock at regular intervals over a fairly long period of time, regardless of the price of the stock. Obviously, you get more shares with your money when the price of the stock is low and fewer when it is high.

And you make a profit if you eventually sell the stock at a higher price than the average price at which you bought it. Table 1 is an example of dollar cost averaging (it does not, for simplicity, take commissions into account and eliminates fractions altogether).

Table 1.   Dollar Cost Averaging

Time	Dollar Amount	Number of Shares	Price per Share
First month	$100	10	$10
Second month	100	9	11
Third month	100	8	12
Fourth month	100	9	11
Fifth month	100	7	14
Sixth month	100	9	11
Seventh month	100	11	9
Eighth month	100	12	8
Ninth month	100	10	10
Tenth month	100	8	12
	$1,000	93	$108

Average price per share: $10.80

In the example, at the end of ten months, you would have bought 93 shares of stock, paying $10.80 per share on the average, and the stock that you paid $1,000 for would be worth $1,116 — 93 times the current price, 12.

Dollar cost averaging isn't a foolproof way of making a profit. It's simply a way of taking advantage of normal price fluctuations instead of worrying about them. But you have to choose a good stock to begin with, and you have to buy it through thick and thin — when the price is down as well as when it is up. Of course, if you decide to sell your stock when the price is lower than the average price you paid, or if your stock goes into a permanent decline and does not recover, you will have a loss. But if the stock you buy has normal price fluctuations but moves generally upward, you will have a profit.

By the end of 1967, the Monthly Investment Plan had been in existence for almost fourteen years, and several hundred thousand accounts had been opened, of which about 250,000 were still in effect. (Some had been terminated, and some people had switched to regular cash accounts.) It seems apparent that one reason for the plan's success was that many Americans recognized the fact that MIP offers a unique combination of automatic dollar cost averaging and paying as you go — plus automatic reinvestment of dividends to make holdings grow faster. It is undoubtedly the simplest form of do-it-yourself investing available.

Clubs for the Clubable

Another popular way for people to get started investing is to form or join an investment club. Suppose you rounded up nine of your friends and you and they agreed to meet once a month and to contribute a set amount of money — $10 or $15 or $20 or more — and invest it in any stock the group agreed to buy, sharing the resulting profits or losses. You would have an investment club.

An investment club may sound like a mutual fund, but it's really quite different. Both require pooling the money of a number of persons, but there the similarity ends. For anyone can buy shares in a mutual fund, but he has nothing to say about the way his money is invested; his funds are managed by professional managers whose fee he helps to pay. An investment club has no professional managers; the members themselves decide what to buy and sell and share in all the decisions as well as the profits and losses. No one who is not an active member participating in the buy and sell decisions is allowed to contribute to the club. An investment club is an amateur organization all the way, while a mutual fund is professional.

People who join investment clubs do so for the purpose of making money, of course — on the theory that two heads are better than one and ten or more are better than two. But an investment club is also an excellent way to learn about investing. In most clubs, each month a different member suggests how the club should invest the month's money. That means he has to know what the stock market is doing, choose from all the stocks available one that he thinks the club should buy, and be prepared to give good reasons for his choice — in effect, to persuade the other members to buy the stock he has chosen. In the discussions of the stock of the month and the regular review of the club's holdings to see whether any should be sold, everyone learns the principles of investing and the language of Wall Street, and everyone keeps up-to-date on the important financial news. An investment club is a good way to have a stake in the economy and a chance to make a profit without investing a great deal of money. Perhaps that is why there are about forty thousand clubs with 139,000 members in the country and why there is a National Association of Investment Clubs at 1300 Washington Boulevard Building in Detroit which puts out a manual on how to start and run a club and has almost ten thousand clubs as members.

9.

Things to Think About Before Buying Your First Stock

Once you've decided that investing is a good idea and are ready to put cash on the barrelhead, what is the next step? Full speed ahead to a broker's office? Dispatch is desirable in most matters, but pause a little while before you invest and consider your financial situation.

Look Before You Leap

First of all, do you have enough money? You don't need a great deal of money in order to invest. As little as $40 will get you started in a Monthly Investment Plan. But before you put any money at all in securities, which, after all, involve taking risks, you should size up your financial situation to be sure that the money you propose to invest is *extra* money and not *essential* money.

That is what we mean. Stock prices, as we know, go up and down unpredictably. That means that you should never buy stock with money that you should be spending somewhere else because you can't be sure of getting back at least as much as you invested (or more) any time you want it. You don't want to be forced to sell your stock at a time when the price is down and you have a loss. You don't want circumstances to dictate your selling time. You want to choose that time yourself when the price is above your purchase price. But you don't know in advance when — if ever — that time will be, and you can't do anything to make it happen. So you see that it is unwise to put money you may need on short notice into stocks.

Things to Consider

Instead, you should do your investing in stocks with extra money that is available after the necessities have been taken care of. What are the necessities? Daily living expenses, of course — food, clothing, shelter, and expenses having to do with education, medical treatment, an automobile, and a certain amount of recreation. It is also advisable to have some cash on hand in case of emergency — an accident, for example, or anything that causes an unforeseeable expense. And anyone with dependents should have some insurance — hospitalization and automobile insurance, of course, and probably also life insurance, accident insurance, and anything else dictated by personal circumstances.

It isn't possible to say what amounts of a family budget should go for these various needs. Obviously, the requirements are different for single people than for families and different for small families than for large ones. According to the Internal Revenue Service, the way the average American family divided its expenditures in 1966 is shown in the pie chart. The "other" category included interest on loans, recreation, education, contributions and medical expenses.

COURTESY OF MERRILL LYNCH, PIERCE, FENNER & SMITH INC.

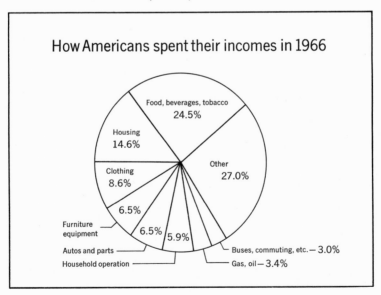

How Americans spent their incomes in 1966

Food, beverages, tobacco 24.5%

Housing 14.6%

Clothing 8.6%

Other 27.0%

6.5%

Furniture equipment

6.5%

5.9%

Autos and parts

Household operation

Buses, commuting, etc. — 3.0%

Gas, oil — 3.4%

Let's assume that you have some extra money after daily living expenses, a cash fund for emergencies, and insurance coverage. The next question you had better ask yourself is whether you are going to be an investor or a speculator. What's the difference?

A Matter of Risk

Basically, the difference is a matter of degree. The investor takes relatively small risks and is content with long-term profits that may or may not be modest. The speculator takes large risks in the hope of making large profits quickly. There is nothing wrong with speculating if you have the temperament as well as the money to tolerate the suspense and the possibility of loss. Just be sure you have!

Fortunately, there is room for both kinds of people in our financial scheme of things. Investors provide capital over the long term to keep businesses going and expanding, and speculators assume risks that investors prefer to avoid and back enterprises that involve more risk. Investors are essentially conservative, and speculators are more daring; both serve their purposes in the financial world as well as serving their own needs.

Most people who buy stocks are investors, taking reasonable risks for reasonable gains. They may secretly wish for big, quick profits, but they know their chances of having them are pretty slim. Let's say you decide that you are an investor. Your next step is to decide on your investment objective. Perhaps that seems odd to you, since everybody invests to make money. But there are different ways of needing money and different ways of making it.

Most people have one of these objectives in mind: safety, income, or growth — or a combination. Actually, people who want *only* a safe place to put their money are likely to put it in a savings bank or into United States Government bonds. In other words, they ignore the loss of purchasing power over the years or feel that it is the price they must pay — and are willing to pay — for safety. In fact, most investors do want safety but don't say so or don't realize it. Nobody wants to lose money, after all. Many people just think that it goes without saying that safety is important to them.

Money Now or Money Later?

What most people *consciously* want when they buy securities is either income or growth. There are essentially two ways of getting income — through interest on bonds or dividends on stocks. In general, individual investors don't buy bonds unless they are very rich, and they don't buy very many preferred stocks, either. When the average investor wants income, he buys common stocks — not just any common stocks but common stocks that pay regular dividends and return 4 percent or 5 percent on the investor's money — $40 or $50 a year for every $1,000 invested. What kinds of stocks are those? They may be stocks in companies in almost any industry. Over the years, many utilities — the companies that supply such basic community needs as light and power and gas — have yielded a steady return to investors that is larger than the average in other fields. And so utility stocks have been popular with investors in search of dividend income.

In general — but there are exceptions — it is older people who want income from their investments. People who are no longer wage-earners may understandably want to supplement their retirement income with dividends.

Younger people are more likely to prefer growth as their

objective, especially if times are good. They probably don't need income and would rather have their investments increase in value over the years. So they buy stocks in companies that are growing faster than the economy as a whole and hope to turn a profit when they sell.

One thing no one should do is buy stocks on a tip — particularly a tip from a stranger. If you stop to think about it, no stranger is going to do you a favor by telling you how to make a profit. If he gives you a tip, he is probably doing *himself* a favor — trying to persuade you to buy something because *he* will benefit, not because *you* will benefit.

It's a good idea to remember that there is no all-purpose stock — no stock that is at once 100 percent safe, guaranteed to pay regular and substantial dividends, and sure to go up steadily in price. If there were such a stock, everyone would own it and no one would own anything else! All you can hope to do when you buy stock is to find a company that will come as close as possible to fitting your needs, whatever they may be.

Finding a Broker

Once you are ready to invest, the wisest thing you can do is go to a reputable broker and open an account with him. If you don't know of a reputable broker, you can ask your bank or your local Better Business Bureau. Or ask a friend whose judgment you trust. Or simply look in the yellow pages for the name of a member firm of the New York Stock Exchange. Why a member firm of the New York Stock Exchange? Because member firms have to meet certain financial and ethical standards, and because the offices of member firms are staffed with men (and a few women) who have passed qualifying examinations about their knowledge of the business given by the New

A broker teaching a course about the stock market to a group of people. PHOTO COURTESY OF MERRILL LYNCH, PIERCE, FENNER & SMITH INC.

York Stock Exchange and the National Association of Securities Dealers and are thus entitled to be called registered representatives. Many of them have taken the formal training program run by the larger brokerage firms or have taken correspondence courses to learn the business. Their courses probably included such subjects as accounting, security analysis, corporation finance, and laws of the securities business, all of which are covered in the exams. Some firms call their registered representatives *account executives,* others call them *customers' brokers,* still others call them *securities salesmen.* But those who do business with the public in a member-firm office are registered representatives no matter what their titles. And you, as a customer, are likely to refer to your registered representative as "my broker" once you have started to do business with him.

10.

What You Should Know When You Open an Account with a Broker: Kinds of Accounts and Orders

When you open an account with a broker, there are several questions he will ask you and some you may want to ask him.

Cash . . .

First of all, he will ask you what kind of account you want to open. Most accounts are cash accounts. You buy securities and pay for them in full, or you sell securities and deliver them, all within five days' time. A Monthly Investment Plan account is a kind of cash account, and so is a joint account, opened by two people (husband and wife, brothers, sisters, friends) who have common ownership rights in the account. There is also a law in every state permitting, in a cash account, gifts of securities to minors with an adult as custodian (since minors cannot own securities solely in their own name).

Custodian . . .

In addition, an investor whose securities are worth a lot of money — say $100,000 or more — may open a custodian account and leave his securities in his own name but with his broker, who will keep them in a vault separated from all other securities.

Discretionary . . .

Another kind of account is the discretionary account, which used to be common but is now much less so; in fact, many brokers will not accept discretionary accounts at all. If you have a discretionary account, you turn over all responsibility for your account to your broker, who buys and sells as he sees fit without consulting you at all — in other words, at his own discretion. As you can imagine, such an account offers an unscrupulous broker an opportunity to take advantage of his customer by buying and selling too often (thus producing more commissions for the broker) or by buying unsuitable securities for his own purposes (to help make the price go up, for example) rather than for the customer's benefit. In investing, it is generally considered much wiser to do it yourself. Or if you don't want to trust your own judgment, hire an investment counselor or buy shares in a good investment company.

Incidentally, the compensation that most registered representatives receive is related, directly or indirectly, to the amount of business they do with their customers. Inevitably, some registered representatives are tempted to increase their compensation by urging their customers to buy and sell more than the best interests of the customers dictate. But the great majority of registered representatives are honest and devoted to their customers' interests. And they know that the penalties for "churning" are severe and that the regulations of the securities business are all designed for the protection of the investor.

Margin . . .

There is one other major kind of account. It is used more by speculators than by investors because it involves taking big risks in the hope of making big gains — but with the possibility of big losses as well. It is called a margin account, and it enables the speculator to buy stocks (usually only the stocks of big corporations listed on the New York Stock Exchange or American Stock Exchange, but that may change) by paying only part of the purchase price and borrowing the rest of the cost of the stock from his broker. In effect, a margin account is a credit account, with the holder of the account owing money to his broker. The proportion of the cost of the stock that the speculator must pay when he buys is set by the Federal Reserve Board and changes from time to time as the FRB seeks to regulate the amount of money in circulation in the country. For example, if you had bought $10,000 worth of stock on margin on January 15, 1963, you would have had to pay $5,000 and you could have borrowed the other $5,000 from your broker because the initial margin requirement at that time was 50 percent. If you had bought $10,000 worth of stock on April 30, 1965, you would have had to pay $7,000 and you could have borrowed only $3,000 from your broker because the requirement was then 70 percent. Since World War II, the initial margin requirement has varied from 50 percent to 100 percent. When the requirement is 100 percent, in effect no margin buying is permitted and you have to pay the full cost of any purchase.

When you buy stock on margin, you are required not only to pay a certain percent of the purchase price. You must also always maintain a certain ownership interest in your stock regardless of the way it fluctuates in price. The New York Stock Exchange has a rule that your equity (your ownership interest) must be at least 25 percent of the value of the stock, and some brokerage houses require even more.

The reason a speculator buys stock on margin is that by so doing, he can increase his purchasing power. He can buy more stock than he could afford to buy otherwise. He pays his broker the standard commission on all the stock he buys on margin (not just on the 50 percent or 70 percent or whatever percent he pays for himself) plus interest on the money he borrows from the broker. And he gets all the capital gains and dividends — if any — on the total amount. The only amount he has to pay back to the broker when he sells is the amount he borrowed plus the interest on that amount.

Pros and Cons

Buying on margin sounds like a good way to increase your profits, doesn't it? It can be that — if your stock goes up in price and stays up. But remember what we said earlier about risk? Wherever there is a possibility of great profit, there is also a risk of great loss. If a speculator buys stock on margin and that stock goes down, he may lose everything — the money he put up, the money he borrowed from his broker, the interest, and the stock itself. And regardless of how the stock behaves, he still has to repay his broker in full.

Here's the proof in the form of two examples (with commissions and interest costs omitted for simplicity): Let's say that a speculator buys 200 shares of a stock at 50, putting down $7,000 in cash and borrowing $3,000 from his broker, for a total of $10,000. If his $50 stock goes to $70 and he sells it there, he gets $14,000, repays the broker $3,000, and pockets $11,000, for a profit of $4,000. (If he had bought $7,000 worth of the stock in a cash account, he would have made a profit of $2,800.)

But — and it's a big but — suppose our speculator had bought 200 shares of a $50 stock, paying $7,000 and borrowing $3,000 for a total of $10,000. And suppose that the stock had dropped in price 20 points instead of rising 20 points, and he had sold it at 30. Then he would get only $6,000 and he would still have to repay his broker $3,000. He would be left with only $3,000 of the $7,000 that he put up originally. (On the other hand, if he had bought $7,000 worth of his stock in a cash account and had sold it at 30, he would have had $4,200 — still less than he put in but $1,200 more than the $3,000 he would have left after buying on margin.)

In theory, it is possible to lose one's whole purchase and then some in a margin account. But because of the New York Stock Exchange rule about margin maintenance, before that happens the speculator would receive a margin call from his broker. A margin call is a request for him to put up more money. If he were unable to meet the margin call, the broker would probably sell the stock and take the amount due him and return the remainder — if any — to the speculator, whose loss would be considerable.

Why do the Federal Reserve Board and the New York Stock Exchange regulate margin? Basically, because of the lesson of the 1920's. At that time, there was no FRB and there were no New York Stock Exchange regulations about the amount of credit a broker could extend to a customer. Many people, in their eagerness for profits, bought stocks by paying as little as 10 percent of the purchase price, bought far more than they could really afford, and couldn't meet their margin calls when prices fell. Their brokers were forced to sell their stocks — only to find there were no buyers. One of the chief causes of the stock market collapse of 1929 was excessive margin buying, which resulted in too many sellers and too few buyers as prices declined.

Selling Short: What Is It?

There is another kind of speculating that can be done only in a margin account, and it is called *short selling*. When a speculator sells short, he sells a stock he doesn't own and then — since he has to deliver to the buyer any stock that he sells — he borrows the appropriate number of shares of the stock from his broker to make delivery. The speculator who is selling short must pay standard commission charges plus interest based on the total amount of money involved. Eventually, the speculator will have to buy the stock in order to return it to his broker, from whom he borrowed it. There is an old Wall Street saying: "He who sells what isn't his'n / Must buy it back or go to prison."

Why does a speculator sell short? Because he thinks the price of the stock he sold short will go down, and then he will be able to buy it at a lower price than he sold it short for and return the stock to his broker and make a profit, all at the same time. Of course, he may be wrong about the price of the stock. It may go up instead. But he'll still have to buy it in order to repay his broker. And in that instance, he will lose money. Short selling is the reverse of margin buying. It is selling in the expectation of a decline in price instead of buying in the expectation of a rise in price. And it is just as risky as margin buying, too.

A fairly small percentage of buyers and sellers of stock have margin accounts. Most people are investors rather than speculators and have cash accounts instead of margin accounts.

There Are Orders and Orders

When you open an account with a broker, you will also want to know what kinds of orders you can place with him. For there are different kinds of buy and sell orders.

Most orders are what are called *market orders,* which are orders to buy or sell at the best price available when the order reaches the exchange trading floor or the broker's over-the-counter department. They are executed as soon as possible, always the same day. There are also *limit orders,* which are orders to buy or sell only at a certain price. You will remember how those orders for stocks listed on the New York Stock Exchange are left with the specialist for execution when the price reaches the appropriate point — if it ever does. If it doesn't, the order simply will not be executed. A limit order may be good for a day, a week, a month, or any period of time the investor chooses. Thus if you want to buy 100 shares of a certain stock only if you can get it for $50 a share and only today, you place a day limit order. If you're willing to wait a week or a month or longer, you just tell your broker how long you want your order to be in effect. It's important to cancel such an order if you change your mind about it. Otherwise, the order will be executed and you may have stock you don't want, or you may have sold without wanting to do so. If you are willing to wait indefinitely for the execution of your order, you can place a GTC or *good till canceled order,* which will remain in effect until it is either executed or canceled. On the whole, a market order is likely to be best, since it means acting on information and decisions promptly.

Certificates: Take 'Em or Leave 'Em

When you open an account, your broker will probably ask you whether you want your stock delivered (that is, whether you want a stock certificate representing your ownership interest in the company) or prefer to leave it in street name. You may want to have the certificate; it is a handsome piece of watermarked paper, engraved to discourage forgery, 12 inches by 8 inches, and it crackles like money. If you do take delivery of your certificate, be sure to keep it in a safe place such as a safe-deposit box, because it is valuable, and replacing lost, stolen, or destroyed certificates is costly and time-consuming. On the other hand, for convenience you may decide to leave it in street name, which is to say in your broker's name (you get a receipt to show that you own the stock), and let your broker serve as your liaison with the company. The difference is essentially a matter of convenience. If your stock is registered in your name and you have the certificate, you will receive communications (annual reports, proxy material, dividends) directly from the company. If it is in street name, those communications will reach you by way of your broker.

Consideration is now being given to replacing the traditional stock certificate with a punch card for easier handling.

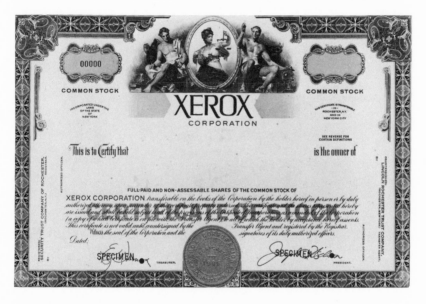

Common-stock certificate of Xerox Corporation. PETER STEINER PHOTO, COURTESY OF XEROX CORPORATION.

11.

·

Where Do You Find Out What You
Need to Know?

One of the things every investor needs to know is how to read
the newspaper stock tables, the columns of daily stock-market
prices, so that he can keep track of the stocks that interest him.
It's easier than it looks. Let's use Jackson Bakery for an example, and let's assume that it's traded over the counter. Most
newspaper over-the-counter quotations are divided into several
sections: industrials and utilities, insurance companies, banks,
and mutual funds — and perhaps foreign securities as well.

Jackson Bakery is an industrial company, so you look for it in alphabetical order in the list of industrials and utilities. There you'll probably find something like this:

	Bid	Asked	Previous Bid
Jackson Bakery 30¢	11	11¾	10⅞

That means that Jackson Bakery stock is currently paying a dividend of 30¢ per share per year; the bid, or the highest price at which buyers were willing to buy, at the time the list was compiled was 11 ($11) and the asked, or the lowest price at which sellers were willing to sell, was 11¾ ($11.75) per share. The previous bid, which is not always included in over-the-counter quotations, is the bid of the preceding business day and is given for purposes of comparison — so that you know whether Jackson Bakery stock is going up or down. But if you want to know the price range for the year, you'll have to look elsewhere — in a publication of one of the financial information services, for example. Or ask your broker.

It's Easy When You Know How

New York Stock Exchange and other stock exchange tables are somewhat more complicated because they include additional information. If Jackson Bakery grew to a substantial size and was qualified and accepted for listing on the New York Stock Exchange, here is how it might appear in alphabetical order under New York Stock Exchange Transactions:

1967 High	Low	Stocks and Dividend in $	Sales in 100's	Open	High	Low	Close	Net Change
53½	44	Jksn Bkry $1.80	35	49½	51	49¼	50	+¼

85

The first two figures, before the name of the company, show the price range for the year. Then comes the name of the company (often abbreviated) with its current annual dividend per share ($1.80). *Sales in 100's* tells you how much of the stock changed hands during the preceding day — 3,500 shares in this instance. *Open* is the first price at which Jackson Bakery Stock was traded on the day in question, *High* is the highest price of the day, and *Low* is the lowest, and *Close* is, of course, the last price of the day on that exchange. (Some companies are listed on more than one exchange.) *Net change* means the price change between the current day's closing price and the preceding day's closing price (not the difference between *Open* and *Close*). And don't overlook the footnotes if they apply to a stock that you're watching; they may be important!

The stock tables can actually tell you quite a bit about a company. For instance, you can compare the current price of Jackson Bakery stock with the *1967 High-Low* figures to see how well it is doing, and you can tell its current trend by taking note of whether the *Net Change* figure is up or down or unchanged. If you watch the *Sales in 100's* figure over a period of time and compare it with the same figure for other stocks, you can tell how actively Jackson Bakery stock is traded in relation to the rest of the stock market. And the dividend figure makes it possible for you to calculate the yield, the return per year expressed as a percent of the price of the stock.

Making Comparisons Easier

You calculate yield by dividing the dividend per year, $1.80, by the closing price, 50. Answer: 3.6 percent, or about average for New York Stock Exchange listed stocks in the 1960's. Good stocks seldom yield more than 6 percent, and some growth stocks yield a very small return or sometimes none at all. Because it is a percentage, the yield figure enables you to compare the dividends paid by various companies with stocks of different prices and dividends of different sizes. You might picture price and dividend as two figures at opposite ends of a seesaw. Assuming that the dividend remains the same, when the price goes up, the yield goes down. And when the price goes down, the yield goes up. Here's how it works:

$$\frac{4.5\% \text{ yield}}{\$40 \text{ price } /\$1.80 \text{ dividend}} \qquad \frac{3\% \text{ yield}}{\$60 \text{ price } /\$1.80 \text{ dividend}}$$

People who read stock tables are usually interested primarily in the behavior of the stocks they own or are thinking of buying. But the price action of your stock alone isn't very meaningful unless you compare it to the behavior of the market as a whole. And for that you need an average, which you'll also find in your daily newspaper.

Averages as Indicators

The best-known stock-market average is the Dow-Jones Average, which is actually four averages made up of the prices of 30 industrial stocks, 20 railroad stocks, 15 utilities, and a combination of all three. The Dow-Jones Industrial Average is what most people mean when they say "the Dow-Jones" or "the average." At the end of 1967, the Dow-Jones Industrial Average was 905.11, somewhat below its all-time high of 995 set in February 1966 but well above its 1967 low of 786.41. The figure is not a dollar figure; it is an abstraction based on stock prices, a way of measuring the performance of certain large companies which are thought to be leaders. The Dow-

Jones Averages are compiled and published several times a day by the company that also publishes *The Wall Street Journal,* a national newspaper with four regional editions devoted entirely to financial news. People who want more investment information than they can find in their local newspapers read *The Wall Street Journal.*

There are two other market averages published in many newspapers. One is a group of averages compiled by Standard & Poor's, the largest and best-known securities research organization in the United States. It consists of a 500-stock composite made up of 425 industrials, 50 utilities, and 25 rails, and like the Dow-Jones, it is published several times each day. Standard & Poor's uses 1941–1943 as its base period with an arbitrary figure of 10. At the end of 1967, it was 96.47.

The New York Stock Exchange also publishes its own average of all the common stocks listed on that exchange and also calculates four other indices for industrial, transportation, utility, and finance stocks. The New York Stock Exchange Common Stock Index, which uses December 31, 1965, as a base with an average price per share of 50, is converted into dollars and cents so that you can say, "Today the average price of a listed stock went up 13 cents" or "down 9 cents" or whatever the appropriate number is. At the end of 1967, the New York Stock Exchange Common Stock Index was 53.83, which means that the average price of all listed common stocks was $53.83.

The American Stock Exchange has its own average also. Besides local newspapers and *The Wall Street Journal,* there are many magazines devoted entirely or partly to business and financial news, including *Barrons, Business Week, Financial World, Forbes,* and *Fortune.* And the major news magazines — *Newsweek, Time, U. S. News & World Report* — carry news

One of the electronic quotation machines in use in many brokerage offices. This one is Telequote 70. PHOTO COURTESY OF THE BUNKER-RAMO CORPORATION.

of the financial world. You'll find them on most newsstands or in public libraries.

What You'll Find in Your Broker's Office

Helpful as all these materials are, when you are looking for investment information, your best source is often your broker. All brokers are equipped to supply up-to-the-minute quotations (more recent than the newspapers' daily quotations). They have several sources: the ticker tape and the quotation board in the office and several kinds of electronic equipment. The ticker tape is usually projected in some form on a screen in a broker's office. Once upon a time, every broker's office had a ticker tape machine (invented by Thomas Edison and introduced in 1867) that reported changing stock prices on a continuous strip of paper seven-eighths of an inch wide — the kind of tape that used to be thrown out the windows of buildings on lower Broadway in New York City when celebrities paraded up the avenue. Now you may find cellophane tape that is projected on a screen. There is also another kind of screen that carries the same information in moving lights without using any ticker tape at all. It's still called "the tape" or "the ticker," but it is actually a kind of electronic sign.

The quotation board in a broker's office also carries changing stock prices. And many brokerage offices are now equipped with electronic devices that look like adding machines on which you punch keys and current information about a security appears on a small screen or printed on a narrow tape as if by magic. These electronic devices are beginning to replace the familiar clicking quotation boards, just as electronic quotation boards once replaced older boards on which clerks wrote changing prices in chalk.

Quotation board in a brokerage office, with projected ticker tape.
PHOTO COURTESY OF MERRILL LYNCH, PIERCE, FENNER & SMITH INC.

You Can't Tell the Stocks Without . . .

To make sense of the information on these various kinds of
equipment, you need to know the symbols for the various
stocks — plus a few other things. The symbols are simply ab-

breviations, because whole company names are too long for convenience. Here are the symbols for the ten companies (all listed on the New York Stock Exchange) with the largest number of stockholders:

American Telephone &		U. S. Steel	X
Telegraph	T	Ford	F
General Motors	GM	Bethlehem Steel	BS
Standard Oil (New Jersey)	J	International Business	
General Electric	GE	Machines	IBM
General Telephone &		E. I. du Pont de Nemours	DD
Electronics	GEN		

Here is the way ticker tape looks on a screen in a broker's office:

IBM   GE   T   J   X   DDP   GM   F   BS

6|5   5s95⅝   50¾   1000s64½   3s40¾   8| 9s83¾   53¾   3

The figures following the International Business Machines, American Telephone and Telegraph, Ford, and Bethlehem Steel symbols mean that 100 shares of each stock changed hands at the prices indicated. Whenever a figure appears alone, it means 100 shares (a round lot). Note also that 100 shares of Du Pont were traded — but the Pr after the Du Pont symbol means that preferred stock, not common, changed hands. Common stock is always meant unless preferred is specifically indicated. The figures 5s95⅝ after General Electric means that 500 shares of GE changed hands at $64\frac{1}{2}$. (5s means 500 shares and 3s means 300 shares and 9s means 900 shares. But note that 1000s means 1000 shares and is written out for clarity after the symbol for Standard Oil of New Jersey.)

The New York Stock Exchange has 900-character-per-minute tickers in operation to speed information all over the country, but even so, the ticker sometimes falls behind trading on very busy days. When it does, even more abbreviations are used in order to save time.

Information Galore

Your broker is likely to be a very helpful source of investment information as well as quotations. Most brokers have some basic booklets about investing available to anyone who asks for them, and they can also supply information about specific securities. Some even have research departments that will give investment suggestions to anyone who tells them his financial situation and objectives and the amount of money he has to invest. Such services are generally free, but brokers offer them in the hope of doing business with the people who request them, which is reasonable enough.

There is another way to get information about any company that interests you, and that is simply to write to the company and ask for its annual report, the financial report that the company prepares for its stockholders each year. Annual reports come in all sizes and shapes from a few mimeographed sheets to elaborate booklets printed in color and containing enormous amounts of information — not only financial information but information about the company's products and management and operations and subsidiaries (if it has any) and even its plans for the future.

12.

Things to Consider When Choosing a Stock

Although a company's annual report can give you a good deal of useful investment information, there are lots of other things you ought to know about a company in which you are thinking of buying stock — things that you won't find in the annual report. Here, for example, are some of the questions you might well ask about the industry as a whole and the company in which you are interested:

Sticky Questions

Does the company provide products or services that are widely used and needed — products or services for which there is a continuing, a growing, demand?

How does the company stand in its industry? Is its competitive position strong?

Is the company's business cyclical? That is, is it subject to major ups and downs, or is it relatively stable? Steel, for example, is a cyclical industry; the demand for steel varies from season to season and from year to year among the industry's biggest customers, the automobile manufacturers and the construction industry. Public utilities, on the other hand, are relatively stable. The fact that an industry is cyclical doesn't mean that you shouldn't buy stock in a company in that industry — but it does mean that you should try to buy the stock at a low point in the cycle and sell it at a high point.

Does the demand for the company's products vary seasonally, or does it vary greatly with general business conditions? For example, a company that makes snowplows has a market for its products only in winter — a precarious position to be in. Wise management is likely to introduce other products, to diversify the company's output, so that it manufactures and markets lawn mowers, too, or some other product with a peak demand in summer. Diversifying markets can help, too. For example, the manufacturer of snowplows might sell his product in South America during our summer — assuming that it is possible and profitable to do so. Stocks in companies that have a steady demand in times of recession as well as prosperity are called defensive stocks. One obvious example is food stocks — stocks in food processing, manufacturing, distributing, and selling. The reason, of course, is that people always have to eat. They may change their eating habits from time to time, but they eat all the same.

War and Peace

What about the effects of war or peace on a stock? Companies that are in the business of manufacturing war materiel or any kind of military supplies are likely to be very profitable during wartime and less so in peacetime — unless they also make other goods. For example, a company that makes fighter planes for the armed services may be able to switch to making passenger planes when the war is over. All industries are subject to some degree to the effects of war and peace. During World War II, virtually no civilian goods were manufactured, so of course the demand for them was tremendous when the war was over.

What is the labor situation in the industry and in the company? Frequent or prolonged strikes have a very unfavorable effect on a company's earnings and therefore on its desirability as an investment.

Is the industry or the company likely to be adversely affected by international news developments? A company may depend on a supplier of raw materials in a country that may be taken over by a coup, or it may have an important market in such a country.

"R & D"

Is the company working steadily to develop new products and improve old ones? Is it strong in what Wall Street calls "R & D" — research and development? Among the industries in which R & D looms large are aerospace, drugs, electronics, and office equipment, but virtually all industries devote some attention to research regarding products or processes or packaging or marketing or some other aspect of their business. In 1967, about $24 billion was spent on R & D, 63 percent by the federal government and 33 percent by industry and the rest by universities and foundations.

In addition to developing new products and improving old ones, is the company seeking new uses and new markets for its products? Some companies undertake programs of public education to encourage the use of their products. For example, the makers of silver and china offer information on the uses of their products to high school home-economics teachers who in turn use that information in their courses. In a more direct way, a company may place publicity stories and advertise uses for consumer products. Think of the magazine articles or television commercials you have seen on the many uses of Scotch tape or Scott towels or some other product. Such efforts cannot be casual or occasional if a company expects to keep or improve its share of its market. If a company is not expanding, it is usually doomed; like Alice in Wonderland, it has to run fast just to stand still. The reason, of course, is competition.

The Big Wheels

How good is management? That is one of the hardest of all questions to answer, because an investor or prospective investor rarely has any personal knowledge of the company's officers. The skill of management can usually be judged only indirectly by the success of the company. More specifically, if a company's labor costs or raw material costs or equipment costs are too high to be economical, that fact is likely to be an unfavorable commentary on management. A well-run company is, of course, a favorable commentary. If you read financial news regularly, you will soon get an idea of the reputations of various company officers. But the best evidence of their skill will always be the company's record in terms of sales, earnings, and dividends and the way in which the company grows over the years. Management is also largely responsible for whether facilities are modern and efficient, whether quality control is maintained, and whether there is overproduction or underproduction of goods for the market. In addition, a well-run company will have not only a capable management team but a strong staff of younger executives waiting in the wings and also the kind of company policies that will attract capable younger personnel.

Then there is the question of ownership management. Is it a good thing or a bad thing? There is no answer to that question. Some people who are large stockholders in their own companies work hard and effectively for themselves and their stockholders, while others regard their stock ownership as a guarantee of income and security and coast along without much thought for the company's future. The latter are becoming rarer and rarer, partly because other stockholders either use their influence to force management to better efforts or else sell their stock, whereupon the price is likely to go down, warning management to pay more attention to the needs of the company.

Who are the directors of the company? They are not employees of the corporation, although the top officers of a company (chairman, president, president of the executive committee) may be directors also. Directors are usually well-regarded men and women who hold high positions in companies that are not in competition with the companies of which they are directors. Thus a bank president might be a director of a steel company, and a steel company chairman might be a director of a supermarket chain, and so forth. Directors usually meet at regular intervals to establish the basic policies of the corporation and to supervise financial planning. They are also responsible for deciding whether or not dividends should be paid, depending on the corporation's earnings and its plans for the future. Directors usually serve without pay — or at least without salary, although some large corporations give their directors token payments for each meeting they attend. Directors are representatives of the company's stockholders and their interests. Sometimes a very large stockholder is himself a member of the board of directors, or a group of large stockholders elect a member to the board of directors to represent their interests.

Other Considerations

Some companies have prospered because they owned valuable patents or processes. Are those patents or processes still valid? Are they about to run out? If they do, where are the company's prospects?

Some industries are regulated by the federal government, and all are affected by it in some ways. Public utilities, airlines, broadcasting, to name three. When the federal government set a limit on the profits of American Telephone & Telegraph in 1967, the price of the stock fell — not surprisingly. Investigations of the profit margins of drug companies often hurt the prices of drug stocks, at least temporarily. Some companies have been found guilty of monopolistic practices and "restraint of trade," and they have often suffered at least temporary setbacks until they revised their way of doing business and made it work.

What is the company's method of marketing its product? If it eliminates the middle man and markets directly through dealers, it may enjoy relatively high prices for its products and its dealers may enjoy good profit margins. On the other hand, aggressive middle men may have considerable influence on the market for a product.

Many investors like to know how many institutions own a company's stock. They think that a stock that is well regarded by the sophisticated investors who manage the investments of banks, insurance companies, pension funds, labor unions, colleges and universities, and corporations is likely to be a good stock. There is a good deal to be said for such unofficial "endorsement," of course, although it's wise to keep in mind the fact that no institution ever falls in love with a stock, as individual investors sometimes do, and therefore holdings of institutions change fairly rapidly.

Is the company promotion-minded? Promotions of various kinds can have a tremendous influence on the popularity of a product or a service. For example, Esso's "Put a tiger in your tank" is credited with increasing substantially the company's share of the gasoline and oil business. Promotions alone seldom have lasting influence, however. They have to be refined or changed from time to time. And it's well to keep in mind that a product or service must live up to the claims made for it or it will lose customers instead of winning them.

Don't Forget Price!

What is the current price of the stock, and what have been its price ranges in recent years? You may say that its past price ranges don't matter because you're interested in the future, but if the stock you have in mind is at or near its all-time high, you may want to think twice before buying it. At least you'll want to consider very carefully whether its future looks as bright as its past before you buy it. It may — and then again it may not.

There are also such factors to consider as the increase in population and, especially in the dominant age groups, the effect of more leisure time and the impact of automation. For instance, when the birth rate is high, companies in the baby product business are likely to boom. A relatively high percentage of older people — plus the effect of Medicare — means an increased demand for drugs and prosperity for drug companies. The shorter work week and the increase in leisure time will probably cause some recreation stocks to rise as people buy things to help them pass the time — sporting goods, games, liquor and soft drinks. Automation is still a great question mark; nobody knows what its impact will be. But already many things are standardized that used to be custom made, and that trend is likely to continue.

Economic Indicators: What on Earth Are They?

Serious investors pay attention to the major economic indicators, which are considered barometers of the stock market, the means by which the climate for investing can be gauged. Among the most important of those indicators are these:

101

GNP

The most basic indicator is probably Gross National Product, or GNP, which is the sum of the value of all the goods and services produced in the country. GNP is calculated by the Department of Commerce and reported quarterly. The figure is meaningful only if you compare it with previous GNP figures to see whether it is rising at a healthy rate. For example, in 1966, GNP was $739.5 billion, an increase of 5.4 percent over 1965. GNP for 1967 was estimated at $785 billion.

FRB

Every month, the Federal Reserve Board reports its Index of Industrial Production, which measures production in industries which produce more than one-third of the nation's income — basic industries such as steel, automobiles, industrial machinery, chemicals, paper products, and electric and gas utilities. The FRB Index is quoted as a percentage of the base period 1957–1959, which is 100. In mid-1967, it was 155.5.

When compared with previous figures, both GNP and the FRB Index indicate whether production is rising or falling and at what rate, and thus they give investors a good idea of the general health of the economy and whether it is improving, remaining pretty much the same, or declining.

BLS

Another important indicator is employment — or, to look at it negatively, unemployment. Figures on employment are compiled and reported monthly by the Bureau of Labor Statistics.

At any given time, there are, of course, some people who are unemployed in the country (other than children, retired people, invalids, and housewives, whose "production" isn't measured). Some are between jobs, some have just entered the labor market and haven't yet found jobs, and some will probably drift along without jobs indefinitely. The unemployment rate usually averages somewhere between 3.5 percent and 4 percent of the labor force of over 70,000,000 even when the economy is healthy. When it runs higher, there is great concern because it is evident that industry is unable to provide jobs for all who want and need them. Further than that, unemployment directly affects the market for consumer goods and indirectly for all goods. Obviously, when employment is high, people tend to spend more for both necessities and luxuries than they do when employment is low and they must tighten the family purse strings.

D. of C.

Disposable personal income, reported quarterly by the Department of Commerce, includes wages, salaries, dividends, and interest for the whole country after taxes, and it is regarded as a good indicator of people's ability to buy goods and services. From 1950 to 1960, disposable personal income rose from $207,000,000,000 to $334,000,000,000, an increase of 61 percent. In mid-1967, it was up to $529,000,000,000.

There is, of course, a relationship among the indicators. For example, GNP reflects industrial production, which in turn reflects employment, which has a great deal to do with disposable personal income.

And Others

All of these indicators are reported on the financial pages of major newspapers and in many business publications and brokers' letters. And there are many other indicators which sophisticated investors watch. Their names are self-explanatory. Among them are

> Steel, automobile, petroleum, and paperboard production
> Electric power output
> Wholesale price index
> Freight carloadings
> Average work-week in manufacturing
> Consumer price index
> Housing starts and new construction
> New orders of durable goods
> Retail sales
> Value of the dollar
> Corporate profits before tax
> Plant and equipment spending
> Business failures
> Installment credit
> Inventories

And in addition to all those indicators, there is the availability of money for the use of local governments, corporations, and individuals. And that is best indicated by the Federal Reserve Board's activities in raising or lowering the discount rate to make money "tight" and relatively expensive or "easy" and relatively inexpensive to borrow.

On the One Hand . . . on the Other Hand

The list of questions could go on and on. And the answers are seldom simple. What is good for one company may be bad for another; what is good for a company at one time may be bad at another time. Everything changes constantly. As a result, no investment decision should ever be final. In investing, as in other matters, it is important to keep an open mind and be willing to change your course of action whenever it seems called for.

But you are probably wondering how you can possibly get all the information you need to make an intelligent investment decision about a company — when you would find the time and where you would find the facts. Ask your broker. Part of his business is providing information about securities as well as buying and selling them. If he is doing his job well, he can probably supply you with a report on any company of any considerable size — either a report compiled by his own firm's research department or one prepared by one of the information services that specialize in compiling such information for investors.

The Future Is a Question Mark

Remember that even the most comprehensive and accurate information and the best judgment do not guarantee success in the stock market. The element of risk remains. "The best laid plans o' mice and men gang aft agley." No one can anticipate some of the events that affect the stock market. The assassination of President Kennedy was unforeseen and caused the market to drop suddenly. The wise investor knows that he is always somewhat at the mercy of unknown factors. That is part of the frustration of the stock market — and its fascination, too. Always remember what J. P. Morgan said when he was asked to predict what the stock market would do: "It will fluctuate."

13.

Annual Meetings and Annual Reports:
What Good Are They?

We've said that one of the privileges of share-owners in a company is that of receiving regular reports on the company's financial condition. The most important of those is the annual report, which the company issues at the end of its fiscal or bookkeeping year and distributes to all of its stockholders. The annual report may contain a balance sheet and an income statement and very little more, or it may be an elaborate and colorful presentation of the company's operations and achievements and products and plans for the future.

Corporate Democracy in Action

The annual report is generally sent to stockholders a short time before the company's annual meeting, to which all stockholders are invited. At about the same time — sometimes in the same envelope — a proxy statement is sent to each stockholder. The proxy statement contains a list of matters of company business on which stockholders are asked to vote — such matters as the election of company directors, a change in the by-laws of the corporation, the terms of a stock-option plan for officers or a pension plan for employees, the selection of the company's auditors, issuing additional stock, or merging with another company.

If you are a stockholder, you are asked to vote either for or against management's recommendations by marking your proxy, which is a kind of absentee ballot, *yes* or *no* on each question and returning it to be counted. You get one vote for each share of stock you own.

If you expect to attend the annual meeting, you may wait and cast your ballot in person at the meeting. In corporate democracy, as in American democracy, you are given the opportunity of voting on issues and candidates that affect your welfare, and some people take the trouble to vote and some don't. If you don't vote, your vote will automatically be cast for management's choice. Occasionally there is a proxy fight as a result of dissatisfaction among a company's large stockholders or the desire of someone outside the company to take it over. Then stockholders are wooed in the hope of winning their votes, and sometimes there are major changes in the company as a result of proxy battles.

Once a Year

Annual meetings vary as much as annual reports do. Some are big and bright and run as smoothly as Broadway productions. Others are small and short. Most large corporations now try to hold their meetings where as many stockholders as possible can attend, moving from one big city to another in different parts of the country from year to year and offering such inducements to attend as special exhibits, local transportation, and box lunches. But some companies still prefer to make it hard for stockholders to attend and hold their meetings in out-of-the-way places. Delaware is a favorite and has a certain logic because many corporations are incorporated in the state of Delaware and can use that fact as an excuse for holding their meetings there.

While most annual meetings are cut-and-dried, taking care of company business fairly briskly and including a report from the company's chairman or president on company activities during the preceding year and prospects for the coming year, very often the proceedings are enlivened by questions from stockholders who are present. They may ask pertinent — or impertinent — questions, such as, Why aren't dividends bigger? Why are there no women on the board of directors? Why is the company giving so much money to charity, or why isn't it giving more? When is a new product or service expected to start showing a profit?

Major company meetings are often reported in newspaper financial pages, and a few companies (such as IBM and Xerox) even issue reports on their annual meetings for stockholders, telling them what action was taken during the meeting.

To return to the subject of the annual report, obviously you'll find it interesting reading if you own stock in the company. And the annual report is also an excellent source of information for anyone who is thinking of buying that company's stock and wants to know more before he does so. As we've said before, you should never buy a pig in a poke. Translated into stock market lingo, that means never buy a stock that you don't know anything about. Find out all you can before you invest your money in a company's stock. And for that purpose, one of your best sources of information about a company is the company's annual report, prepared by the company for its stockholders. (Between issues of the annual report, current facts and figures about the company are available from brokers or from information services such as Standard & Poor's.)

What You'll Find in an Annual Report

The balance sheet and financial statement are the heart of the annual report. Although they may look confusing at first glance, they are far from being a meaningless bunch of figures. They contain much of the information you need to judge a company's soundness. Let's take a look at the balance sheet of a fictitious company called Red, White & Blue Corporation.

First of all, it's important to know that a balance sheet tells you how a company stands as of a certain date, usually the last day of its fiscal (bookkeeping) year and in the case of Red, White & Blue the last day of 1967. That's why a balance sheet is sometimes called a statement of condition as of a certain date. The second thing you'll notice at once is that a balance sheet comes in two sections and always balances; that is, total assets always equal total liabilities. Assets are plus factors, and liabilities are minus factors.

Plus and Minus

The balance sheet exists because companies use so-called double-entry bookkeeping. In double-entry bookkeeping, every item is entered twice, once in the debit column (liabilities or *minus* figures) and once in the credit column (assets or *plus* figures). Thus if a customer of the company pays for goods received, the amount of the payment is added to the credit column and subtracted from the debit column. On the other hand, if the company pays a supplier for raw materials, the amount of the company's payment is subtracted from the credit column and added to the debit column. The columns are always in balance, and the company's management can tell at any time how the company stands by looking at the balance sheet, which is a summary of all the bookkeeping entries.

Current Ratio

But what specific information can you get from a balance sheet that you need before investing? Well, you may wonder if a company has enough working capital for its needs, enough money to carry on its business efficiently. To find out, you simply divide the current assets by the current liabilities: $7,000,-000 \div \$3,000,000 = 2.3$. The answer is called the current ratio, and it means that Red, White & Blue Corporation has 2.3 times as much in assets (plus factors) as in liabilities (minus factors), which is a good healthy proportion. In general, the current ratio should be at least 2 to 1 for manufacturing companies, less for service companies which do not carry large inventories of goods.

111

Red, White & Blue Corporation

Balance Sheet or Statement of Condition as of December 31, 1967

Assets (amounts owned by or owed to the company)

Current Assets

Cash		$2,000,000
Accounts receivable (amounts owed to the company by its customers)	$2,100,000	
Less provision for bad debts	100,000	2,000,000
Inventories (raw materials and finished goods)		3,000,000
Total current assets		7,000,000

Property, Plant & Equipment (fixed assets)

Land	150,000	
Buildings	3,000,000	
Machinery	1,000,000	
Office equipment	500,000	
	4,650,000	
Less accumulated depreciation	2,000,000	
Net property, plant & equipment		2,650,000
Deferred charges		100,000
Good will, patents, trademarks		200,000
Net Assets		$9,950,000

Liabilities (amounts owed by the company)

Current Liabilities

Accounts payable (amounts owed by the company for wages, raw materials, etc.)	$1,500,000	
Notes payable (amounts borrowed by the company)	1,000,000	
Accrued expenses payable	100,000	
Income taxes payable	400,000	
Total current liabilities		3,000,000

Long-term Liabilities

First mortgage bonds 5 percent interest, due 1980		2,500,000
Total liabilities		5,500,000

Stockholders' Equity

Common stock, $5 par value, authorized, issued & outstanding 500,000 shares	2,500,000	
Retained earnings (profits kept by the company for future use)	1,950,000	
Total stockholders' equity		4,450,000*

Total Liabilities and
Stockholders' Equity $9,950,000

* You may wonder why stockholders' equity is considered a liability or *minus* factor instead of an asset or *plus* factor. To put it as simply as possible, it is because the company does not own the stockholders' stock; the stockholders own it.

Quick Assets

You can also find out the company's quick assets, the assets that can be turned into cash readily, by subtracting inventories from total current assets ($7,000,000 − $3,000,000 = $4,000,-000) and dividing this figure by the current liabilities (4,000,-000 ÷ 3,000,000 = 1.3). The answer, 1.3 to 1, is the quick asset ratio. Then you know that the company has $1.3 in assets available to meet each $1 of current liabilities. In general, that ratio should be over 1 for most companies.

Book Value

Then there's net book value, the value behind each share of the company's stock. To find it, you take the company's total tangible assets (no intangibles such as goodwill, patents, or trademarks), subtract its liabilities, and divide by the number of shares of common stock outstanding so that you get the figure on a per-share basis, thus: $9,950,000 assets − $200,000 goodwill, etc. = $9,750,000 − $5,500,000 liabilities = $4,250,-000 ÷ 500,000 shares = $8.50 book value.

Book value has nothing whatever to do with market value, but it is interesting for two reasons. One is that it is often considered to be the liquidation value of the company, the amount of money that would be realized if the company were to go out of business and sell all of its tangible assets. (Whether it would *actually* realize that much money is a good question. Do you ever receive full value if you sell something second hand?) The second thing to keep in mind about net book value is that it is useful chiefly for purposes of comparison with the same company's book value over the years to see whether the company is gaining or losing ground in terms of the value of its property.

Capitalization

The balance sheet also tells you the company's capitalization, the total amount of securities of all kinds that it has outstanding. When you know the company's capitalization, you can calculate the capitalization ratio or equity-to-debt ratio, the proportion of the company's bonds (debt) to its stock (equity). To get it, you simply take the current *market* value of the common stock — not the stockholders' equity but the number of shares shown on the balance sheet (500,000) — and multiply by the current price of the stock from today's newspaper (let's say it's $20) and then divide the answer, $10,000,000, by the face value of the bonds as shown on the balance sheet, $2,500,-000. The answer is 4, and it tells you that the value of Red, White & Blue Corporation's stock is four times the value of its bonds. A ratio of up to 5 to 1 is considered reasonable for a manufacturing company.

Why should you be interested in the equity-to-debt ratio? Because it's generally unwise to buy stock in a company that has a much greater value of bonds than stock outstanding. Remember that bondholders take precedence over stockholders in every way, and if there are too many bonds outstanding on which interest must be paid, the stockholders may never get any dividends at all.

Leverage

To be more specific, if bonds constitute a very large proportion of a company's capitalization, the company is said to be leveraged and its stock may be considered relatively unattractive.

115

The reason is that interest on bonds must be paid before any dividends can be paid on stock, and if bond interest takes most of the company's earnings, there will be little or nothing left for dividends on the stock.

On the other hand, if earnings are very good, a substantial amount will be available for dividends. To put it another way, when earnings of a highly leveraged company are good, dividends on the common stock are likely to be good, and when earnings are bad, dividends may be small or may be omitted altogether. So if you think earnings will be good, the stock of a highly leveraged company may be a good buy — and of course the opposite is true, too.

The Income Statement

Now let's consider the other set of facts and figures readily available about Red, White & Blue Corporation, the income statement, sometimes called the statement of profit and loss because it tells how much money the company made or lost in a certain period of time, usually its fiscal year. We'll look at the income statement of Red, White & Blue for the year 1967.

Red, White & Blue Corporation

Income Statement for 1967

*Net sales		$8,000,000
Cost of sales and operating expenses		
Cost of goods sold	$5,000,000	
Depreciation	1,000,000	
Selling and administrative expenses	500,000	6,500,000

Operating income	1,500,000
Other income	
Dividends and interest	+150,000
Total income	1,650,000
Other deductions	
Interest on bonds	—125,000
Income before taxes (gross income)	1,525,000
Provision for taxes	—525,000
Net income for the year	$1,000,000

* Sometimes called Revenues.

Profits or Earnings . . .

What sort of information do you get from the income statement? First of all, of course, you find out that Red, White & Blue made $1,000,000 in 1967 after paying all its expenses, including taxes. It sounds like a lot of money on the face of it, but let's see if it really is — all things considered.

. . . per Share

First of all, you want to know the company's earnings *per share,* the amount of money that the company made for each share of its stock. (*Net income* and *earnings* are interchangeable terms; both in effect mean profit.) So you divide net income, $1,000,000, by the number of shares of stock outstanding, which you get from the balance sheet, 500,000, and you learn that Red, White & Blue Corporation earned $2 per share in 1967. That doesn't, of course, mean that every stockholder

117

automatically receives $2 for each share of stock that he owns in the company. But it does mean that the company's board of directors will probably declare dividends of about 50¢ over the year, and also that there will be money left over to put back into the company for expansion and development — new products, new equipment, new markets.

P/E Ratio

Another piece of information that you can get from the financial statement is the company's price-earnings ratio, sometimes called its P/E ratio. That is, as its name implies, the ratio of the current price of the stock from the daily newspaper, $20, to its earnings per share for the year, $2. When you divide the current market price by the earnings per share, you get the figure 10 (10 to 1), which means that Red, White & Blue stock is selling at ten times earnings, ten times the profit (per share) for the year. The figure, of course, changes when earnings change, and also when the price of the stock changes, as it does frequently. There is no absolute standard for the price-earnings ratio, no magic number that means a healthy company. At the end of 1967, the price-earnings ratio of the thirty companies in the Dow-Jones Industrial Average was 17.2/1. A price-earnings ratio of 10 is considered quite low. For a growth company, the price-earnings ratio may go to 35 or 40 or even higher. Like so many of the other figures we have been discussing, price-earnings ratio is less meaningful in itself than it is when compared with other figures — in this instance, with the company's price-earnings ratio in earlier years and with the price-earnings ratios of other companies in the same industry and with those in other industries.

Margin of Profit

You also want to know what the company's margin or profit is, the ratio of the profit from its operations to its net sales, the amount of money that it makes on the goods that it sells. So you divide operating income ($1,500,000) by net sales ($8,000,000), and the answer is 18.75. What does it mean? Margin of profit ratios vary a great deal from industry to industry, being relatively low in such fields as food manufacturing and distributing and relatively high in such fields as cosmetics, so it's hard to say exactly what a healthy margin of profit ratio is. But generally speaking, it should be 15 percent to 30 percent, depending on the industry. If possible, it's always a good idea to compare this figure over a period of years to see whether the company is improving its margin of profit ratio by more efficient methods. If it has to work harder to make the same profit, something may be wrong — its costs may be too high or its efficiency too low — and a competitor may come along and win away the company's customers.

Some companies make some of these calculations for you and provide tables of historical information about the company in each annual report. Most tell you about the company's products or services and its plans for the future. If the company owns other companies, figures on those other companies will probably be included as part of a consolidated balance sheet. And there is usually information about the company's directors in the annual report. (Remember that it is the stockholders of a company who elect the directors.)

Depreciation and Depletion

Then there's a sizable item — $1,000,000 — called depreciation. You probably know what the word means in a general sense — a decline in the value of an item because of age, obsolescence, or wear and tear. An automobile, for example, depreciates with use and the passage of time. In accounting, the term depreciation is applied only to fixed assets (assets that stay in one place) such as buildings, machinery, tools, and the like. Depreciation is important because it represents one of the chief sources of capital for expansion and improvement. (The other sources are borrowing, selling securities to the public, and retaining company earnings instead of paying them all out in the form of dividends.) How can that be? The reason depreciation represents capital for the corporation is that the Internal Revenue Service considers depreciation an operating cost which is *not taxable*. And because depreciation is not taxable, and fixed assets do not have to be replaced until they are worn out, the figure for depreciation gives you a good idea of the amount of money available to the company immediately for its use.

Similar to depreciation is an item called depletion, which appears in the financial statements of companies which use natural resources as the raw materials of their business — oil, metal ore, and timber, for example. Because they consume those irreplaceable assets and destroy them by using them, the Internal Revenue Service permits such companies a depletion allowance based on the percentage of the estimated value of the natural resource used. Thus the corporation's taxable income is reduced, and it has more capital at its disposal to use for its own purposes.

Know Your Company

You may wonder why it is necessary to know all these things about a company before you buy its stock. There is no law that says you must, of course. But the Securities and Exchange Commission was created partly to make sure that plenty of accurate information about companies is available to investors and prospective investors. And it's common sense to know what you're buying before you buy it, just as you would want to know as much as possible about any other important purchase before putting your money down.

Look at it this way. If you were buying a business, you would certainly want to know all you could about that business. You would want to know how much the business would cost you and how much money you could expect to make on it in a year's time — in other words, the price-earnings ratio. You would want to know what the company owned (its assets) and how much it owed (its liabilities) and how many bonds and stocks it had outstanding so that you would know how much interest would have to be paid each year and how many stockholders would have to be considered and whether they were accustomed to being paid dividends. You would want to know how efficiently the company was operating, and one quick way to find out would be to look at its margin of profit ratio. In short, you would want to know the whole story about the company.

Well, when you buy stock in a company, you are buying the company — not the whole company but a part of it. And since you are buying stock with the idea of making a profit, you want to know what the company's chances are of making money and how much. That's why knowledgeable investors find that a careful study of balance sheets and income statements is worthwhile.

14.

How to Fit Your Stocks to Your Aims

Every investor is a case unto himself. His circumstances are unique. But his investment objective is likely to be similar to that of other investors, since there are really only four basic objectives: safety, income, long-term growth with relatively low risk, and short-term growth with relatively high risk (through speculation).

Safety First, Last, and Always

Everyone who buys securities is interested in safety, sometimes without realizing it, because everyone invests for the sake of making money, not losing it. If safety is of primary importance and all else is secondary, the investor should probably buy U. S. Government bonds or good quality corporate bonds. For example, an elderly man might buy bonds simply to preserve his estate for his children, especially if he thought the outlook for business was not bright enough to justify buying stocks instead.

Money Coming In

Income is likely to be of interest chiefly to older people — to retired couples and to widows and widowers. Take the case of Mr. and Mrs. John J. Their children are grown and self-supporting. They own the house they live in. John J is retired from his job as a buyer for a mail-order company. He has a pension of $7,500 per year plus Social Security, and an insurance policy pays him an annuity of $1,500 per year. Medicare helps protect the J's from major medical expenditures. Mr. and Mrs. J can live in reasonable comfort, but they would like to be able to travel a bit and to do things for their young grandchildren. So they might buy stock in several good utility companies, where they know their savings will be reasonably safe and they can count on dividends of more than 4 percent a year and perhaps a little growth as well. Those dividends enable them to visit their grandchildren and indulge them occasionally.

The Most Popular Objective

Long-term growth is the objective of most investors. Not that they wouldn't prefer short-term growth, but they are reluctant to assume the greater risk involved in trying to make money quickly.

Take Kate A, for example. She is twenty-three and single and teaches school in a Midwestern town. Her salary is $5,000 a year. She is engaged to a young man who is in medical school, and they expect to be married when he finishes. Meanwhile, she wants to save as much as she can to help them set up housekeeping when the time comes. Her brother, who is a businessman, suggests that she set aside $75 a month and invest it for long-term growth. Kate should keep a small savings account for emergencies, but she doesn't need a great deal because she has no dependents and her health is good and her job includes health insurance coverage. So at the suggestion of a local broker, she starts to buy stock under the Monthly Investment Plan, where her dividends will be reinvested automatically and where there is no penalty if she has to skip a payment some month. The question is, what stock or stocks should Kate buy? Many people make their first investments in fields about which they have some personal knowledge, even in the companies for which they work. Knowing about the increase in the number of young people of school age and the vast sums appropriated by the federal government for education, Kate might choose to invest in a company that specializes in textbooks and other educational materials. Or she might consider stock in a drug company or a manufacturer of hospital supplies, since she knows from her fiancé of the great developments under way in those fields. Both are growth industries and therefore good for her purposes.

What about Mr. and Mrs. James K? They are in their mid-thirties and have two children. They own their house, and he has good insurance coverage. James K earns $15,000 a year as an engineer, but it goes for the expenses of the family household plus payments on the family house and the car. When Betty K inherits $5,000 from an uncle, the K's might decide to invest it for the children's education. Obviously, they want the money to grow as much as it can with safety. They are less interested in dividends because James K's salary takes care of their immedite needs. What should they do with the $5,000 that Betty K inherited?

Because he is an engineer, James K keeps up with new scientific and industrial developments. He sees the impact of automation on all kinds of business, and he thinks that it might be wise to buy stock in a company that makes computers or computer supplies. He also believes that companies which are helping to solve the problems of air and water pollution have a bright future. The question is, should the K's invest the whole $5,000 in one stock, or should they divide it among several stocks?

The K's wisely decide to discuss their problem with a broker, and their broker tells them that there are two sides to the question of diversification. If an investor spreads his money among too many different companies, especially if his total investment is a relatively small amount of money, he spends too much in commissions. Further than that, he reduces the risk of investing — but at the cost of also reducing his chance of making a substantial profit. Suppose, for example, that you were to divide your investment between two stocks, and one did well and the other did poorly. You would undoubtedly wish

that you had put all your money in the stock that did well —
but at the same time you would be relieved that you hadn't
put it all in the stock that did poorly. The broker's advice to
the James K's in this instance was to invest half of the money
in a good company in the computer field and half in either air
or water pollution control.

Speculating the Wrong Way and the Right Way

Consider also the case of George S, a young man, single, earn-
ing about $12,000 a year as a salesman. He has no dependents
and no plans for marriage at the moment. He runs into an old
school friend on the street one day, and the friend brags to him
about the "killing" he has just made in the market. His stocks
turn out to be speculations in so-called penny stocks (low-
priced stocks, usually costing less than $2 or $3 a share) in uranium mines and small manufacturers of far-fetched products.
George S says to himself, "Why shouldn't I make some money
that way, too?"

Fortunately, George S first discusses the matter with a
broker who tells him that his friend was probably exaggerat-
ing, because only about one penny stock in a hundred or more
ever makes a profit for people who buy it. And he reminds
George S that his friend didn't mention any losses, although
he almost certainly had some. The broker agrees that since
George S has no dependents, he can afford to speculate, but
instead of uranium stocks, he suggests a company that is important in both commercial aviation and the space program
plus a small, new company in electronics.

These are, of course, only a few possibilities among thousands. All of the people we've told about have a good chance of
making profits on their investments because they chose with

care, keeping in mind their own circumstances and sizing up the nature of each company and its prospects with the help of a broker. Also they kept their expectations reasonable, knowing that very, very few people ever get rich quick in the stock market — or anywhere else.

Following a Formula

Some people believe in investing according to a formula in order to benefit from price fluctuations — they hope. For example, they may divide the money they have to invest into two parts and use one part to buy stocks and keep the other part in cash with the idea of keeping the same dollar amount of stock all the time. Naturally, they sell stock when the price is high and buy more with the cash fund when the price is low.

Another formula plan is to make the same division of funds into two parts, one for stock and the other for cash, and always keep the same dollar value of stocks in proportion to cash — 50–50 or 60–40 or whatever. People who use this formula sell when their stock rises beyond a certain point and put the proceeds into the cash fund. And, of course, when the price of the stock falls below a certain point, they buy more out of the cash fund.

There are other formula plans, too. Do they work? Nobody knows for sure. They may have worked for some people at least some of the time, but there are no records available to the public to show whether formula investing is generally profitable or not. Formula investing requires watching the performance of the stocks closely and acting promptly when the occasion arises, and very few people are attentive enough and decisive enough to do both.

Don't Fall in Love

Buying stock is not the solution to everyone's financial problems — far from it. It's only the beginning. One thing every investor should recognize and remember is this fact: No investment decision is ever final. Or as Bernard Baruch put it, "There ain't no such animal as a permanent investment." Circumstances change, and the prospects for stocks change all the time. So it is important for an investor to follow the performance of his stocks regularly to see whether they meet his requirements — do as he expects them to do. And if they don't, he must always be willing to change his mind and his holdings. Nobody is right all the time, so no investor should let himself fall in love with a stock or tell himself that it will turn out all right if he just holds on long enough.

Onward and Upward

A wise investor keeps himself informed of the news about his company and other companies in the same industry as well as on general business conditions. He reads his companies' annual reports and quarterly reports, and he checks price performance in the newspaper at least once a week. He consults with his broker whenever he has a question about his stock, and he has his holdings reviewed by his broker's research department every year or so to get an objective opinion on what he owns.

Most important of all, he is just as willing to sell as he is to buy. Instead of watching a stock that he owns fall indefinitely, he sells it and buys something else. By weeding out, he improves the quality and the performance of his holdings. And when he has a stock that is moving upward, he holds it as long as it continues in that direction. That does not mean that he is in and out of stocks all the time. Many investors have made handsome profits by buying certain stocks and holding them for years — but the stocks were usually good stocks to begin with. But remember that a paper profit or a paper loss is just that — paper. It doesn't count to anyone — not to you, not to the Internal Revenue Service — until it is a *real* profit or a *real* loss.

Some investors are reluctant to take short-term profits because they must pay higher income tax on short-term gains than on long-term gains — generally speaking, twice as high. (Short term, by definition of the Internal Revenue Service, is six months or less.) Others are reluctant to take large long-term gains because they may have to give as much as 25 percent of their profit to Uncle Sam. They are said to be "locked in" — even though nobody is locking them in but themselves. Actually, it is never wise to make an investment decision for a tax reason alone. If it is time to sell a stock, it is time to sell, and you are likely to be better off selling than holding. You might lose more by holding on than by selling and paying the tax on a short-term gain. Similarly, it is foolish to stay locked in when you might better sell, pay the tax, and invest your money elsewhere.

Whys and Wherefores of Selling

There are, of course, almost as many reasons for selling a stock as there are investors, and we can't possibly enumerate them all here. A disappointing performance is only one of them — though it is an important one. An investor may also sell because he thinks a stock has risen as far as it is going to rise for a

130

while, or because he needs the money for some other purpose, or because he has found another stock that he thinks is even better than the one he owns. Your personal circumstances may change, too, and with them, your investment needs. For example, when a single man marries, he is likely to change from speculative stocks to more conservative issues for long-term growth. A growing family may change his objectives, too. And when he retires, the chances are he'll be more interested in income than growth. All these changes of circumstances call for changes in investments, too.

There are also external reasons having nothing to do with the investor and his personal circumstances. For example, no matter how thoroughly an investor has acquainted himself with the facts about a company and its stock, unforeseen — and unforeseeable — developments can change the outlook for the company. Congress or a government agency may pass a law or make a ruling that will affect a company's prospects. One of the most obvious examples is the federal budget, on which all military spending depends and which is controlled by Congress. A cut in the military budget may mean that some projects will be discontinued and others never undertaken, and the companies concerned will be affected accordingly. An unexpected news development can also affect the stock market — the outbreak of a war, the illness or death of a President, all kinds of domestic and international developments. Scientific discoveries may have an impact on certain kinds of stock. A change in the discount rate may affect others. Even a broker's report on a stock may affect its price, at least temporarily, and so, of course, may a company's own announcement of a new product or a change in management or a proposed merger or an increase or decrease in earnings.

Some factors are harder to describe. One is public opinion.

131

There are stocks which have increased in price far more than stocks which are comparable to them in every way, and the reason — as far as anyone can tell — is simply that some stocks catch the public fancy and others don't.

Surprise Reaction

Strangely enough, there are times when a stock or a group of stocks may not respond to a piece of news as you would expect. Ordinarily, if a military contract is canceled, you would expect the stock of the affected company to drop. But the stock may not drop in price; it may stay the same or even rise. The reason is that investors have already taken the possibility of the cancellation into consideration and think the company's long-term prospects are still good. When that happens, it is said that the market (meaning investors) discounted the news.

In short, buying stocks is only half the battle. Knowing when to hold and when to sell is equally important. And everything is subject to change without notice.

A Few Words About Selling

A few more words about selling may be in order. Many people buy stock only to be disappointed by its performance, and often they hold on and hope for better things instead of selling it and buying something else. It is foolish to be either stubborn or sentimental in the stock market. Two of the worst things a investor can do are (1) hold on to a disappointing stock because he doesn't want to admit that he made a mistake in choosing it, and (2) hold on to a disappointing stock because he has an emotional attachment to it, because he has "fallen in love with it."

In the first place, there is no loss of face in selling a stock at a loss. Nobody can possibly be right all the time. If you buy a stock that does what you want it to do, by all means stay with it. If it doesn't do what you want it to do, after a reasonable period of time, don't hesitate to sell it. And don't be sentimental when you invest. A stock is not a person. There are no obligations or attachments where stocks are concerned — no reasons not to cut your losses. Buying a company's stock is not the same as endorsing the company or its products. Investment decisions should be made for such cold-blooded reasons as earnings and research and prospects.

In selling, as in buying, you should keep your wits about you. For example, we mentioned yield earlier. If a stock is yielding 7 percent, which is considerably higher than the average, that yield may be either a good reason to buy the stock or a good reason to sell it. Before you make any investment decision, you had better find out whether the price is relatively low or the dividend is relatively high and why.

And here's something else to keep in mind when you read reports on stocks. If you buy a stock at 40 and it rises to 80, it has gone up 100 percent. If you buy a stock at 80 and it falls to 40, it has gone down only 50 percent. Yet the number of points is the same, in both instances. A report on a stock can be written to make the stock's performance look better or worse by using such comparisons, so always be sure you understand what is being said literally as well as by implication.

133

15.

Things That Can Happen While You
Hold a Stock

There is no such thing as status quo in the stock market. Everything is changing all the time. So when you buy stock, you must not expect anything to stay as it was when you bought it — not the price, not the dividends, not the management, not the products or markets, not the world situation. Here are some of the things you can expect to happen when you own stock.

Ex = Without

It goes without saying that the price of your stock will fluctuate — a little or a lot depending on other investors' opinions of the company's prospects. The dividend — if there is any — can change, too. Remember, a company is not obliged to pay dividends at all, even if it has done so in the past. That decision is up to the directors, who are likely to make their decision on the basis of the company's earnings.

When it comes time for the dividend on your stock to be paid, you may notice that the price of your stock drops. The reason is that anyone buying the stock at that time won't get the dividend. The stock is said to have gone *ex dividend,* which means without dividend, regardless of what you may have learned in Latin. Ex dividend is xD in the stock tables in the newspaper.

Here's what happens. Let's say the directors declare a dividend of 50¢ a share payable to all stockholders of record on the company's books on July 10. The dividend won't actually be paid until July 25, but it will be paid to those who owned the stock on July 10. If you own the stock on the record date, naturally you will get the dividend on July 25 or thereabouts. But if you buy the stock on July 6, 7, 8, 9, or 10, you won't get the dividend — although you will probably pay a half point or 50¢ a share less for your stock. The reason is this: Five days are allowed for settlement of purchases and sales of stock. That means you have five days to pay for a stock you have bought or to deliver the certificate for a stock you have sold. When a dividend is declared, the stock goes ex dividend for four days before the record date plus the record date itself. Reason: If you buy the stock during those four days, you can't become a

135

stockholder on the record date, so you're *not* entitled to the dividend. (If you sell during that time, of course you *are* entitled to the dividend.) Here's how it works, step by step:

June 25: Directors declare dividend of 50¢ per share payable to stockholders of record July 10.

July 6, 7, 8, 9, 10: Stock goes ex dividend and price declines one-half point (50¢).

July 25: Stockholders who owned the stock on July 10 get dividend of 50¢ per share.

Another Kind of Dividend

There's another kind of dividend that the directors may declare, and that is a stock dividend — additional shares of the company's stock in proportion to the shares you already own. For example, they may declare that each stockholder of record on a certain date will receive one share for every 25 shares held.

But what if you own 10 shares and get only two-fifths of a share. Or what if you own 80 shares and get three and one-fifth shares. There's no such thing as a fraction of a share. So what happens? The chances are your broker will call you to ask you if you want to sell the fraction at the market price or round out the share — that is, pay for the three-fifths or four-fifths to make a full share. Whatever you decide to do, you'll probably have to act within a certain specified period of time, because the company will set a deadline for selling or rounding out.

Should you sell or round out? If you can afford it at the time, you should probably round out. Why? Because it's a good way to increase your holdings, assuming that you think the company is a good one and is going places. If you don't think so, you shouldn't hold the stock at all; you should sell it.

What Is a Right?

We mentioned earlier that when a company that already has stockholders decides to issue more stock to raise additional funds, it often offers the new stock to its present stockholders first at an advantageous price somewhere below the market price. It does this by issuing rights (also known as subscription rights) to its present stockholders in proportion to the shares each one holds. For example, if Jackson Bakery stock were selling at 50, the stock might be offered to stockholders at 48. The company does this by issuing what are called rights. You as a stockholder have the choice of using your rights and buying more stock or of asking your broker to sell your rights, which have a market value, before the deadline or expiration date. Some people let rights lapse without taking any action at all, which is foolish. To keep that from happening, some brokerage houses automatically sell unexercised rights on which they have no instructions just before the deadline and credit their customers' accounts accordingly.

A warrant is similar to a right except that it usually has a longer life — months, years, even forever. Thus if you buy a warrant, or another kind of security that has a warrant attached to it, you are entitled to buy the company's stock at a certain price for the life of the warrant — which is good if the price of the stock goes above that price and bad if it doesn't.

Splits

Suppose you own 50 shares of a stock that has risen to $90 a share, and your company thinks that it would like to increase

137

stockholder interest by getting the price of the stock down to a level where more investors can afford to buy 100 shares. Obviously, the company decides, with the permission of its present stockholders, to split the stock two for one, two shares for each one held (or it might be three for one or four for one or three for two or any other way). Then each stockholder automatically owns twice as many shares as before, and each share is worth half as much. You own 100 shares worth $45 a share instead of 50 shares worth $90 each, in that case. Your proportionate share of ownership in the company remains the same.

Sometimes the price of a stock rises after a split, sometimes it falls. Sometimes the dividend is increased, sometimes it stays the same. (It is rarely decreased.) Unquestionably, a stock split calls attention to a company and often stimulates investor interest. But it doesn't automatically increase the value of the stock, although it may have that effect in the long run.

Looking Ahead

From time to time as you read the stock tables in the newspaper, you'll see the letters *wi* near the name of a company. Those letters mean *when issued* and refer to stock that has been authorized but isn't actually for sale yet, sometimes stock on which a proposed split has been announced. Investors are buying and selling it in anticipation of its being issued, and no transactions are final until the stock is actually issued. The when-issued price of the stock is usually pretty close to the price of the stock that is already on the market.

Tender Offers

In Wall Street, a *tender offer* is not a proposal of marriage, although it may be a step toward a merger. Let's say that a big company wants to diversify its operations by acquiring another company in a different field. One way of doing so is to approach the other company's management with an offer to buy, to negotiate terms, and to present them to the stockholders of both companies for approval.

Another way is the so-called take-over, which is a kind of back-door way of acquiring a company whose officers and directors may not want to sell. Let's say that the big company decides to buy enough of the smaller company's stock to get control of the company. Naturally, it has to buy that stock from the smaller company's stockholders. It may do so over a period of time in the open market. But suppose it wants to acquire the smaller company as quickly as possible. It may advertise to present stockholders that it will buy a certain number of shares before a certain date and at a specified price, which must, of course, be attractive to those stockholders and therefore is likely to be above the current market price.

Such an offer to buy shares is called a *request for tenders*. Stockholders of the smaller company then have a choice before them: to hold their stock or to make a tender offer — that is, to offer to sell it to the big company. Sometimes the management of the smaller company advises stockholders where it thinks their best interest lies. Many stockholders ask their brokers about the merits of the request for tenders. Whether the big company succeeds in its take-over bid depends entirely on the smaller company's stockholders. Take-over bids are fairly common these days, so no stockholder should be surprised if a company in which he owns stock is on one end or the other of a take-over bid sometime.

Mergers and consolidations are frequent, too. In a merger, one company takes over one or more others. In a consolidation, two or more companies get together and a new company is formed. Among those that you may have heard about in recent years are the acquisition of Avis by International Telephone and Telegraph and of Hertz and Random House by Radio Corporation of America and the mergers of McDonnell and Douglas Aircraft and of the New York Central and Pennsylvania Railroads.

Spinning Off

Sometimes the reverse of an acquisition happens, and a corporation which owns smaller companies called subsidiaries distributes the stock of a subsidiary to its stockholders in what is called a *spin-off*. The stockholders are already owners of the subsidiary as well as of the parent company, so the stock doesn't cost them any money. What's the point? Usually a parent company spins off a subsidiary because the government has brought or is about to bring antitrust action against the parent company for having a monopoly that restrains competition in a certain kind of business. And if the parent company gets rid of the subsidiary, it ceases to have a monopoly and no longer is subject to an antitrust suit by the government.

Puts and Calls, Whatever They May Be

Here's another situation altogether. Let's say you are a speculator and have a strong conviction about the price you think a stock will sell for at some time in the future. Then you may want to buy a put or a call — a put if you already own the stock, and a call if you don't. Puts and calls are options, and an option is a right to sell or buy a piece of property at a stated price within a stated period of time. A *put* is an option to sell, and a *call* is an option to buy.

Suppose you are a speculator and you own 100 shares of Super Corporation stock, which you bought at 15 and which is currently selling at 25. You think the stock is going down, but you're not sure, and you want to protect your profit. So you buy a put, an option to sell 100 shares of Super Corporation stock at 25 within ninety days. That means that you can sell your stock at 25 any time within the next ninety days, regardless of the way the stock behaves. For this privilege, naturally, you pay a fee — let's say $175. If Super Corporation stock goes down, you exercise your option, sell the stock at 25, and consider the cost of the put to be money well spent to protect your profit.

What happens if the stock goes up? You don't exercise your put but simply watch your stock rise and regard the cost of the put as insurance and tell yourself that it's part of the price of speculating. If you never exercise your option, you write off the cost to your own peace of mind.

A call works in just the opposite way, guaranteeing the purchase price of a stock for a certain period of time, usually 60 or 90 or 180 days, the same time periods generally in use for puts.

Generally speaking, puts and calls are available only on stocks listed on the New York or American Stock Exchanges. They can be bought, often through brokers, from dealers who specialize in them, most of whom are in New York City. (Puts and calls are illegal in some states.) The terms vary with the quality of the stock (terms on relatively stable stocks of big corporations being generally more favorable than on stocks with a tendency to fluctuate a great deal), its price, and the length of the option.

Exterior of the New York Stock Exchange from the steps of the Sub-Treasury Building at Wall and Broad Streets in downtown New York.

16.

What Is an Exchange and What Goes on There?

The over-the-counter market (sometimes called the unlisted market) is the biggest securities market in the country, but it is less well known than another securities market, the so-called listed market held in marketplaces called exchanges. There are stock exchanges in many free-enterprise countries, and there are a dozen of them in the United States: American Stock Exchange (New York), Boston Stock Exchange, Cincinnati Stock Exchange, Detroit Stock Exchange, Midwest Stock

In 1792 a group of brokers founded the New York Stock Exchange under a buttonwood tree on Wall Street in New York. PHOTO COURTESY OF THE NEW YORK STOCK EXCHANGE, BASED ON EXHIBIT IN THE MUSEUM OF THE CITY OF NEW YORK.

Exchange (Chicago), National Stock Exchange (New York), New York Stock Exchange, Pacific Coast Stock Exchange (trading floors in Los Angeles and San Francisco), Philadelphia-Baltimore-Washington Stock Exchange (trading floor in Philadelphia), Pittsburgh Stock Exchange, Salt Lake City Stock Exchange, Spokane Stock Exchange.

The Giant of Them All

By far the largest in terms of the value of stock traded there is the New York Stock Exchange (often called the Big Board) at the corner of Wall and Broad streets in the downtown area of New York City. On the floor of the New York Stock Exchange, the stocks of more than twelve hundred corporations are bought and sold — a small number of companies but all large companies, companies which employ about one-fifth of all the civilian workers in the country, which own almost one-third of all the corporate property in the country, which produce a great variety of goods and supply a great variety of services.

The New York Stock Exchange was founded in 1792 to fill a need for a centralized marketplace in which to trade the securities that were issued by the United States Government to pay the costs of the American Revolution and by corporations which were doing business in the new republic — banks, canal companies, insurance companies, utilities, the cotton industry.

Keeping Up with the Times

In the early days, the New York Stock Exchange was a call market — as some European exchanges still are. At eleven-thirty each morning, those who wanted to buy or sell stocks assembled, and an officer of the exchange stood and called off

145

The New York Stock Exchange when it was a call market in the 19th century. PHOTO COURTESY OF THE NEW YORK STOCK EXCHANGE.

the names of all the stocks one by one. As each name was called, the men who wanted to buy or sell that stock did so. By 1871, the list had become much too long for the call procedure, and the system was changed. A large meeting place called a trading floor was built with trading posts placed around it at intervals, and certain stocks were assigned to be traded at each post during buiness hours each day. In that way, the broker who wanted to buy or sell a stock would be able to go to the appropriate trading post at any time during the business day

146

and find other buyers and sellers. Thus the call market gave way to a continuous market. The exchanges in the United States are all continuous markets with trading floors, and they generally do business between 10 A.M. and 3:30 P.M. five days a week.

It is important to keep in mind that the exchanges are simply marketplaces. They do not own stocks, and they do not set prices in any way. It is the law of supply and demand that determines prices and makes them fluctuate. Essentially, an exchange provides two things: a place for buyers and sellers to do business and a price-reporting service to make information on changing prices available to those buyers and sellers and to the general public as well.

Going, Going . . .

The exchanges are auction markets. That is, what is for sale is sold to the highest bidder. All bids and offers are made by open outcry (out loud) so that everyone involved knows exactly what is going on. No secret deals are permitted. But before we go into the matter of exactly what happens on the floor of an exchange, we have to know some other things. We have to know, for example, how a stock exchange is organized and what the rules are.

First of all, you want to know who buys and sells securities on an exchange. The answer to that is only members, men who have met certain personal and financial standards and have applied and been accepted for membership, may do business on an exchange. Membership in an exchange is usually called a "seat," and it may have been an appropriate name in the old days of the call market, but it certainly isn't appropriate anymore. Very few people sit down less than members of the exchanges, who are on their feet most of the working day. The number of seats (memberships) on each exchange is limited, so a man who wants to own a seat has to buy it from someone who already owns one or from the estate of a member who has died. The New York Stock Exchange, for example, has 1,366 members who paid different prices for their seats. The price of a seat, like the price of a stock, depends on supply and demand, and supply and demand in turn depend on the amount of trading on the exchange and on how good general business conditions are. Early in 1968, a seat was sold for $475,000.

Belonging Comes High

In the boom of 1929, the price of a seat on the New York Stock Exchange went as high as $620,000. In 1942, when World War II was going on and trading was light, it was down to $17,000. During 1967, the range was $197,000 to $445,000.

There are five kinds of memberships in the New York Stock Exchange. Each kind entitles the owner to do business on the Exchange, but each kind of member does business in a somewhat different way — but all under the rules and the roof of the Exchange. Of the New York Exchange's 1,366 memberships, about 650 are held in the names of member firms, brokerage houses which buy and sell securities for their customers, the investors of the United States. Those 650 members do business for the general public. They are usually called *floor brokers.* Like other members, they must file certain financial information with the Exchange and submit to an annual surprise audit. And they must carry a fidelity bond to protect their customers against any fraud or dishonesty on the part of employees.

Of the other members, over 100 are called *$2 brokers,* and

they transact business for the brokerage houses when brokerage house floor brokers have more business than they can handle. The $2 broker got his name in the days when he received $2 for every order he executed. Now he is compensated on a sliding scale depending on the amount of money involved, but he is still usually called a $2 broker.

A small number of seats — fifteen to twenty — is owned by *registered traders,* men who buy and sell securities primarily for themselves and who don't do business with the public at all. About 125 seats are owned by brokers who act for the odd-lot houses. And what, you may ask, is an odd lot? Quite simply, on the New York Stock Exchange stocks are bought and sold in packages, so to speak. The usual unit of trading, or package, is 100 shares of a stock, and 100 shares is called a round lot. Any number smaller than 100 is an odd lot. (On a very few relatively inactive stocks, a round lot is 10 shares and an odd lot is 1 to 9 shares.) When an investor wants to buy or sell fewer than 100 shares of a stock, his floor broker executes the order through one of the two odd-lot dealers with representatives on the floor of the New York Stock Exchange.

Somewhere between 350 and 400 seats are owned by *specialists,* men who serve two functions: They execute orders for other brokers in the stock or stocks in which they specialize, and they maintain orderly markets in those stocks. We'll talk more about the specialist in the next chapter.

These 1,300 plus men (there are no women doing business on the floor of the New York Stock Exchange — yet — although one woman owns a seat) are the only ones who can buy and sell securities on the New York Stock Exchange. If you want to buy or sell securities on the New York Stock Exchange, you have to get one of them to do it for you. That's easier than it may sound. It doesn't mean that you have to travel to New

149

A group of floor brokers and a specialist (with notebook) on the floor of the New York Stock Exchange. PHOTO COURTESY OF THE NEW YORK STOCK EXCHANGE.

York and go to the Exchange and call on one of the floor brokers to buy or sell stock for you. But it does mean that you have to buy or sell through a member firm of the New York Stock Exchange — one of the 647 firms with one or more floor brokers at the Exchange. Those firms have 4,130 offices all over the country to take investors' orders, and they have more than 42,000 registered representatives, men and women who have passed examinations to test their knowledge of the securities business and who are in the offices of member firms in all fifty states to serve you.

What's on the Market?

What securities are bought and sold on an exchange? Only the stocks that have applied to those exchanges, have met the standards set by the exchanges, and have been accepted for trading there. About 4,000 to 5,000 American corporations have their stock traded on some exchange, and some are traded on more than one. When a corporation's securities have been accepted for trading, they are said to be *listed* on an exchange. Strictly speaking, it is the securities that are listed, not the company; but people often talk about "listed companies."

What must a company do to have securities listed? It must file a registration statement with the SEC so that the financial facts about the company are on record. Then it must apply to the exchange for the listing of its securities. Listing doesn't happen automatically.

Meeting the Requirements

The New York Stock Exchange, the largest of the exchanges, has the strictest listing requirements. A company that wants to

151

have its securities traded there must prove that it is a going concern of good standing in its field and that it has national investor interest. Further than that, the company wishing to have its securities listed must meet these qualifications:

1. The company must be worth at least $10,000,000.

2. The company must have earned at least $1.2 million a year after taxes.

3. The company must have at least 1,000,000 shares of its stock in the hands of at least 2,000 stockholders — and 1,700 or more of those stockholders must own 100 shares or more.

In addition, any company wishing to have its securities listed on the New York Stock Exchange must agree to send its stockholders annual financial statements so that they know how their company is faring, and every share of common stock must have voting rights so that the stockholders can have a say in company policies and can elect directors to represent them. A stock may be delisted if it fails to meet the listing standards sometime after listing.

There is another requirement for listing, too. Because the financial center of the country is the southern tip of the island of Manhattan, the area that is loosely called Wall Street, the New York Stock Exchange requires that corporations with listed securities must have a registrar and a transfer agent in the Wall Street area. The registrar and the transfer agent are often banks, but a corporation may not use the same bank for both purposes. The *registrar* of the company makes sure that the company does not issue any more securities than it is authorized to issue. (Additional unauthorized shares of stock would, of course, decrease each stockholder's proportionate

152

share of ownership of the company and the value of his stock.) The *transfer agent* keeps a record of the name and address of every stockholder, receives certificates representing shares that have been sold, and issues certificates for shares that have been bought. The registrar audits the work of the transfer agent to be sure that everything is in order.

Why do companies choose to have their stocks listed on the New York Stock Exchange — if they can meet the standards — since it is expensive to do so? There are several reasons. One is prestige. Another is that being listed usually results in having their stock owned by more people, and many corporate executives think that stockholders are also customers and so the company may acquire more customers by being listed. In addition, a listed company may find it easier and more economical to raise additional funds than an unlisted company. Unquestionably, listing provides a broad national market for a company's securities and usually stimulates interest among investors.

From the standpoint of the investor, there are advantages, too. Information about a listed company is easy to find. So is the current price of the company's stock. And if the investor wants to buy — and more important, if he wants to sell — there is a ready market at all times. No one wants to buy a security that he will have trouble selling. It was to meet that need that the New York Stock Exchange was founded back in 1792, and its facilities still provide a ready market for all the stocks that are listed there.

Names and Numbers

How many companies have securities listed on the New York Stock Exchange? Early in 1967, almost 11 billion shares of stock worth $523 billion were listed. The number of companies

153

was about 1,260, including the giants of American industry. Here are two lists of companies whose stock is traded on the New York Stock Exchange. On the left are the companies with the largest aggregate market value at the end of 1966, and on the right are the companies with the largest number of stockholders:

American Telephone & Telegraph	American Telephone & Telegraph
International Business Machines	General Motors
General Motors	Standard Oil (New Jersey)
Standard Oil (New Jersey)	General Electric
Eastman Kodak	General Telephone & Electronics
Texaco	Ford
General Electric	U. S. Steel
Sears, Roebuck	Radio Corporation of America
E. I. du Pont	International Business Machines
Gulf Oil	Bethlehem Steel

The exchanges, then, are associations of brokers who agree to do business with one another in a set place and according to certain rules. And who makes the rules? The members of the New York Stock Exchange elect a board of governors, which sets policy and chooses a president to serve as chief executive officer of the Exchange. The board of governors consists of thirty-three members: three who have no connection at all with the securities business, the chairman and the president of the Exchange, and twenty-eight members from all parts of the country. The Exchange operates under the scrutiny of the Securities and Exchange Commission, which oversees the activities on all of the exchanges.

The actual day-to-day operation of the New York Stock Exchange is handled by the staff under the direction of the president. The New York Stock Exchange has a subsidiary called

154

Stock Clearing Corporation which enables member firms to eliminate much of their paperwork. It means that instead of exchanging actual securities with other firms at the end of a day's trading, a record is kept at Stock Clearing Corporation by computers which match buy and sell reports of member firms and make it unnecessary to exchange physical evidence of security ownership. Other experiments in streamlining the handling of securities are also under way.

Wall Street's Colorful Past

The Wall Street area — just one square mile surrounded on three sides by water at the southern tip of Manhattan — has a long and colorful history. The Italian explorer Verrazano and his men were probably the first Europeans to lay eyes on it, followed by Henry Hudson, for whom the great river was named. But the area wasn't settled until 1625 — only five years after the colony at Plymouth was settled by the Puritans. It was a trading post first, and in a sense it has been one for more than three centuries. A year after the first Dutch settlers arrived, Peter Minuit bought the island of Manhattan from the Indians for $24 worth of trinkets in perhaps the most famous real-estate deal in history.

New York was New Amsterdam and Dutch first, then New York and English, then Dutch again under peg-leg Peter Stuyvesant, then English — until 1783, when the American Revolution drove the British out. The wall that gave Wall Street its name was put up in 1653 to keep the Indians from swooping down on the settlers, and it stood until 1699. Among the famous early citizens of New York were Captain Kidd, who was commissioned to defend English ships against pirates, turned pirate himself, and was hanged in London in 1701, and John Peter Zenger, who established the principle of freedom of the press in a famous trial in 1735.

New York was occupied by the British during most of the American Revolution, but after the colonies won their independence, the city came into its own as the capital of the new country. Thomas Jefferson lived in the Wall Street area for a time, and Alexander Hamilton practiced law there — and was buried in Trinity Churchyard after his death in a duel with Aaron Burr. Washington said farewell to his soldiers at Fraunces Tavern in the Wall Street area, and he took the oath of office as first President of the United States at the Sub-Treasury Building on Wall Street in 1789. He lived nearby and worshiped at St. Paul's Chapel, where his pew is still marked. It was to provide a marketplace for the buying and selling of securities to pay for the American Revolution that twenty-four men met under a buttonwood tree on Wall Street in 1792 and founded the New York Stock Exchange.

The nineteenth century found some distinguished citizens playing parts in Wall Street. Robert Fulton's *Clermont,* the world's first practical steamboat, made its maiden voyage on the Hudson River, and Fulton is buried in Trinity Churchyard. In the 1840's in the Wall Street area, P. T. Barnum operated a museum of freaks, Duncan Phyfe made furniture, Mathew Brady had a photographic studio (twenty years before he made his name taking photographs of the Civil War), and Currier & Ives made and sold the prints that are part of the American heritage of popular art. Long before Ellis Island was made a way station for immigrants from Europe, Castle Clinton, situated in New York's magnificent harbor just south of Manhattan Island, was where they arrived from their long voyage. The first ticker-tape parade up Broadway took place in

Wall Street begins at Trinity Church and ends at the East River in downtown New York.

1867 during the Harrison-Cleveland presidential campaign — and started a tradition.

Wall Street has always been the financial center of the country. It has also always been close to the sea, both literally and figuratively. Ships bound to or from the seven seas still pass through the nearby Hudson River and the harbor. The Fulton Fish Market, the biggest in the country, still sends its wares up and down the Eastern seaboard. Marine supply stores offer ropes and lamps and oilskins to seafaring men. And when the wind blows, you can smell not only the salt of the sea but the aromas of spices and roasting coffee from business establishments that have stood in the Wall Street area for a hundred years and more.

17.

The Biggest Exchange and How It Operates

What happens when someone places an order to buy or sell stock listed on the New York Stock Exchange? Suppose, for example, that over the years Jackson Bakery Corporation has become a big company and is now listed on the New York Stock Exchange, and Joseph Brown, who lives in Boston, decides to buy a round lot, 100 shares, at the market, which means at the best price that prevails when his order reaches the floor of the New York Stock Exchange.

First, Joseph Brown goes to a broker whose firm is a member of the New York Stock Exchange. If he doesn't know a member firm, he looks in the yellow pages of the telephone book under *Stock & Bond Brokers* for member firms of the New York Stock Exchange or he may ask a friend, a lawyer, or a banker. If he doesn't have an account, he opens one by filling out a form giving his name, address, telephone number, age (he must be over twenty-one), Social Security number, business association, and a bank reference. If he does have an account, he may simply call his broker and say, "Please buy 100 shares of Jackson Bakery for me at the market." Most people do business with their brokers by telephone.

Where the Action Is

Joseph Brown's broker immediately sends a wire over his firm's wire system to New York, probably directly to the floor of the New York Stock Exchange. There it is received by the firm's own clerk and given to the firm's floor broker, who takes it as quickly as possible to the trading post on the Exchange floor where Jackson Bakery is traded. The Exchange's trading floor is about two-thirds the size of a football field and likely to have a couple of thousand people on it during trading hours.

Meanwhile, in San Diego, Mrs. Jane Green has decided to sell 100 shares of Jackson Bakery stock that she owns because she wants the money to make a down payment on a beach house. She calls her broker, whose firm is a member of the New York Stock Exchange, and tells him to sell her 100 shares of Jackson Bakery at the market. Like Joseph Brown's broker, he wires the order immediately to the floor of the New York Stock Exchange, and there the order is picked up by his firm's floor broker and taken to the appropriate trading post. Keep in mind now that the buyer wants to buy as low as he can, and the seller wants to sell as high as he can.

Each broker knows — because it's his business to know — the approximate price of Jackson Bakery stock. The last price at which the stock was sold is posted on the trading post, together with a plus or minus sign indicating whether the trend is up or down. Let's say that Mr. Brown's broker arrives at the trading post, notes that the last sale was at $50\frac{1}{8}$ ($\$50.12\frac{1}{2}$ per share), and says, in a loud, clear voice, "How's Jackson Bakery?" Notice that he doesn't indicate whether he wants to buy or sell. But when he says, "How's Jackson Bakery?" other brokers with orders to buy or sell Jackson Bakery — including Mrs. Green's broker, who has just arrived at the trading post — call out their bids to buy or offers to sell Jackson Bakery stock at various prices near the $50\frac{1}{8}$ of the last sale. Everything must be transacted out loud; no secret deals are permitted.

Mr. Brown's broker hears all the bids and offers and realizes that at that moment $50\frac{1}{4}$ is the most that anyone is willing to pay for Jackson Bakery stock and $50\frac{1}{2}$ is the least that anyone is willing to sell it for. He then offers to buy 100 shares at $50\frac{3}{8}$ — $\frac{1}{8}$ more than the highest bid and $\frac{1}{8}$ less than the lowest offer. Mrs. Green's broker promptly says he'll sell 100 shares at $50\frac{3}{8}$, recognizing the fact that he is unlikely to get a better price at that moment for Mrs. Green's shares.

Sold!

The two brokers agree on the price, and each one makes a note of the transaction for his own records. They do not exchange any papers or sign any contracts; their agreement is purely oral. In effect, their word is their bond. A clerk who is an employee of the New York Stock Exchange is present during the transaction and sends a report to the Exchange's ticker room, where it is put on tape and projected in board rooms of brokerage houses all over the country so that investors and brokers know the latest price of the stock.

Mr. Brown's broker reports back to his clerk that 100 shares of Jackson Bakery stock have been bought at $50\frac{3}{8}$, and the clerk wires the information to his firm's office in Boston. Mr. Brown's broker tells Mr. Brown — probably within five minutes of the time when Mr. Brown placed the order, for most transactions in active stocks take only a short time. Mrs. Green's broker does the same, and Mrs. Green is told that she has the money for her beach house. Actually, Mrs. Green has sold 100 shares of stock to Mr. Brown without ever having met him. The sale was accomplished by using the facilities of the New York Stock Exchange with its continuous auction market.

Mr. Brown and Mrs. Green receive printed confirmations of the transaction within a day or two so that they have a record of the number of shares, the price, the commission cost, and any taxes involved. Both keep their confirmation forms for income-tax time. The confirmation form also shows settlement day, which is the day by which Mr. Brown must pay for his stock and Mrs. Green must deliver her certificate. Settlement day is the fifth business day after the transaction on the floor of the New York Stock Exchange.

How Odd Is an Odd Lot?

If Mr. Brown had wanted to buy fewer than 100 shares or Mrs. Green had wanted to sell fewer than 100 shares, the procedure on the floor of the New York Stock Exchange would have been somewhat different, but they would both still get the benefit of the Exchange's auction system. For example, if Mr. Brown wanted to buy 10 shares of Jackson Bakery stock, his broker would send his order to the floor of the New York Stock Exchange in the same way, but there it would be turned over to an odd-lot broker, who would execute it by selling the stock out of his own inventory at the price of the next round-lot transaction in Jackson Bakery stock to reach the Exchange floor. An odd-lot sale would be handled in the same way. The services of the odd-lot dealer cost the buyer or seller an amount of money that is called the *odd-lot differential*. On stocks selling under $55 a share, such as Jackson Bakery, the differential is $\frac{1}{8}$ of a point or $12\frac{1}{2}$¢ per share. On stocks selling at $55 or more, the differential is $\frac{1}{4}$ of a point or 25¢ per share. The odd-lot differential is added to the purchase price or subtracted from the sale price, and the broker's commission is additional. Incidentally, odd-lot transactions do not appear on the ticker tape. And odd-lot dealers do not do business directly with the public.

Costs and How to Figure Them

The cost of buying and selling stocks is based on the amount of money involved (not the price of the stock per share) and ranges from 6 percent on small transactions to about 1 percent on large ones. Table 2 (on page 164) shows the New York Stock Exchange commission rates on round lots that went into effect on March 30, 1959. They apply also to transactions on other exchanges and are used as guidelines in the over-the-counter market as well. A few examples are worked out for you in Table 3.

For odd lots, the rates are the same as for round lots — minus $2 — if the amount is over $100. For examples, see Table 4. There are two exceptions that should be noted. On any transaction above $100, the commission charge must not be larger

Table 2

Amount of Money Involved	*Minimum Commission*
Under $100	As mutually agreed
$100 to $399.99	2% plus $3 ($6 minimum)
$400 to $2,399.99	1% plus $7
$2,400 to $4,999.99	½% plus $19
$5,000 and over	1/10% plus $39 ($75 maximum)

Table 3

Price per Share × 100 Shares		*Calculation*	*Commission per 100 Shares*
$10	$1,000	1% of $1,000 = $10 plus $7	$17
$45	4,500	½% of $4,500 = $22.50 plus $19	$41.50
$70	7,000	1/10% of $7,000 = $7 plus $39	$46

To find the commission on an order for a multiple of 100 shares — 200 or 300, for example — simply multiply the 100-share commission by 2, 3, or the appropriate number.

Table 4

Number of Shares × Price per Share		*Money Involved*		*Minimum Commission*
25	× $20	= $500	1% of $500 = $5 plus $5	$10
50	× $80	= $4,000	½% of $4,000 = $20 plus $17	$37
60	× $150	= $9,000	1/10% of $9,000 = $9 plus $37	$46

164

than $1.50 per share or $75 per transaction. And in any event, on a transaction over $100 the minimum commission is never less than $6 per transaction. Federal and local taxes add a few more cents to the cost of selling stocks.

The View from the Gallery

The procedures as well as the commission rates are much the same on the other exchanges as they are on the New York Stock Exchange. Many of the exchanges have visitors' galleries where you can stand and watch the activity on the trading floor and often hear a talk about what is going on as well. The New York Stock Exchange, for example, has an exhibit hall (with a film) and a visitors' gallery that attracts 600,000 visitors a year. A commentator explains to visitors what the men on the noisy trading floor below the gallery are doing, and visitors can see the trading posts, the brokers and clerks at their work, and the telephone clerks calling their floor brokers by means of giant annunciation boards covered with numbers. The floor is a noisy place, but visitors are sheltered from the din by heavy glass separating them from what's beneath them.

The American Stock Exchange also has a visitors' gallery (with exhibits and a film) overlooking its trading floor at 86 Trinity Place in downtown Manhattan, and the explanatory talk tells you why the place resounds with shouting. The American Stock Exchange was once an outdoor market called the curb market on Broad Street in New York. These brokers did business in securities outdoors in all kinds of weather, and they communicated with their clerks, who were hanging out windows in offices overhead, by means of shouts and a special sign language. Both are still in use, even though the curb market moved indoors in 1921. Tradition dies hard in Wall Street.

165

Trading floor of the New York Stock Exchange. DICK HANLEY PHOTO.

Busy as a Beehive

You won't be surprised at the amount of activity on the floors of the exchanges when you realize how many shares of stock are bought and sold every business day. During 1967, on an average day, about 10,000,000 shares changed hands on the floor of the New York Stock Exchange alone. Five years before, the average volume was 3.8 million, and ten years before, it was 2.2 million. During 1967 and 1968, volume on the New York Stock Exchange was so heavy that trading hours were shortened on several occasions to enable brokerage houses to get caught up on their paper work. The all-time record, 16.4 million shares, which stood for many years, was on October 29, 1929, the day of the stock-market crash that preceded the great Depression of the 1930's. But that record was exceeded several times during 1968, once on April 10 (20.41 million shares) and again on June 13 (21.35 million shares). At the rate the volume is growing, these records will probably fall soon. But there is little danger that prices will fall as much again.

The American Stock Exchange has also had a tenfold increase in its daily trading volume in the ten years from 1957 to 1967. American Stock Exchange volume set a record of 10.8 million shares on June 13, 1968.

Why the great increase? Because more Americans are buying — and selling — stocks than ever before — over 24,000,000 in 1967 compared with about 9,000,000 in 1956 and 17,000,000 in 1962. And because institutions such as banks, insurance companies, investment companies, pension plans, and labor unions are buying and selling more than ever. They hold about one-third of all the stock listed on the New York Stock Exchange and the amount is growing all the time.

In spite of the enormous number of shares that change hands every day on the New York Stock Exchange (and other exchanges as well), it's worth remembering that most shares are being held by investors, not bought and sold. The so-called *turnover rate* on the New York Stock Exchange, the rate at which stock changes hands, was 16 percent in 1965 and 18 percent in 1966 and 23 percent in 1967, and much of it was the result of buying and selling by institutions. So keep in mind that even when the stock market is most active, only a small percent of shares is changing hands.

Incidentally, this may be an appropriate time to say that generally speaking, a company does not make or lose money as its stock rises or falls — unless it owns a large number of its own shares. In the long run, the price of its stock will affect as well as reflect the company's success or lack of it. But remember that it is not the company that is selling the stock that is changing hands on the floor of the exchange. It is other stockholders.

18.

The Special Job of the Specialist

Once you know how the auction system works, it's easy to understand how stocks and some corporate bonds change hands on the floor of the New York Stock Exchange. But wait a minute. It just happened that when Mrs. Green wanted to sell 100 shares of Jackson Bakery, Mr. Brown wanted to buy. What if somebody wanted to buy when there was no seller or sell when there was no buyer. Would the buyer or seller have to wait — perhaps for days?

The answer is no, and the reason is the specialist, who is a special kind of member of the Exchange and who, like the odd-lot broker, does business only with other members and not with the general public at all. The specialist (there are 350 to 400 of them) stands at one trading post all day and does business only in one stock or in a group of stocks. If you stand in the visitors' gallery at the New York Stock Exchange, you can spot the specialists because they stay close to one trading post, they wear distinctive badges (as do all members and employees of the New York Stock Exchange), and they keep long, narrow record books close at hand all the time.

Job Specifications

The rules of the New York Stock Exchange describe the specialist's job this way:

He must effectively execute orders which are entrusted to him by other members of the Exchange. He must maintain, insofar as is reasonably practicable, fair and orderly markets on the Exchange in the stocks which he services by dealing for his own account.

Here's how it works. Take the first sentence first.

Suppose that Mr. Brown had told his broker in Boston that he wanted to buy 100 shares of Jackson Bakery — but only if he could get it for $50 a share, slightly lower than the current market price. That kind of order is known as a limit order. Mr. Brown's broker would send the order to the New York Stock Exchange in the usual way — but marked LIMIT — and his firm's floor broker would take it to the appropriate trading post, just as with a market order. If the floor broker found that the current price was slightly higher than the price on Mr. Brown's limit order, obviously he could not simply stand around

171

at the post and wait for the stock to drop to 50 — which it might never do anyway. So he would turn the order over to the specialist, who would write it in his book (a page is reproduced here), where he also keeps a record of other brokers' orders to buy or sell stock at prices away from the current market. He enters orders for the stock in which he specializes in the order in which he receives them and crosses them off as he executes them. (This record-keeping is done by hand now, but there's a good possibility that it may be done by computer in the future.)

What happens is this: When Jackson Bakery stock sells at 50, the specialist executes Mr. Brown's order and sends a report to Mr. Brown's floor broker so that he in turn can see that Mr. Brown is notified that his order has been filled at 50. For acting as a broker's broker, the specialist is paid a commission by Mr. Brown's broker. But Mr. Brown doesn't have to pay anything over the regular commission charge just because his order was executed by the specialist rather than by his floor broker. The floor broker's firm pays the specialist out of the commission that Mr. Brown pays.

That's one example of the first part of the specialist's responsibility. The second part is more complicated. In order to maintain fair and orderly markets, the specialist must own at least twenty trading units (generally speaking, 2,000 shares) of any stock in which he specializes and must be willing and able to buy shares at a higher price than anyone is willing to pay and to sell shares at a lower price than anyone is willing to take. In other words, he must have capital and be willing to risk it in the performance of his job.

For example, when Mr. Brown bought his shares of Jackson Bakery from Mrs. Green, there was only one-quarter of a point between the highest price that anyone was willing to pay at

A page from a specialist's notebook. COURTESY OF MERRILL LYNCH, PIERCE, FENNER & SMITH INC.

that moment and the lowest price that anyone was willing to sell for. But if the difference had been somewhat greater, if for some reason it had been two points, the specialist would have stepped in and bid or offered for his own account at a price close to that of the last transaction. In that way, he would help keep the price of the stock from seesawing wildly. Normally, about 15 percent of the trading volume on the New York Stock Exchange represents specialists' purchases and sales for their own account.

Going Out on a Limb

The specialists on the floor of the New York Stock Exchange are at their posts every trading day, but their importance is shown most clearly in times of emergency when some news event causes stock prices to fall sharply. For example, on September 25, 1955, President Eisenhower had a heart attack. The next day when the stock market opened, sell orders far outnumbered buy orders. So the specialists stepped in and made almost one-quarter of the purchases that day for their own accounts — 1,759,360 shares with an estimated market value of $80 million. As things turned out, the market recovered and the specialists made profits on their purchases. But they had no way of knowing that would happen when they stepped in to help prevent a disastrous slide in prices. They performed the same function on November 22, 1963, when President Kennedy was assassinated and sell orders greatly outnumbered buy orders and prices began to slide. On that day, in the twenty-seven minutes between the announcement of the assassination and the closing of the Exchange, 570,000 shares of twenty-five key stocks were traded — and the specialists bought 140,000 of them in a falling market.

Now of course the specialists are in business to make money, just like everyone else, and to do that they have to have profitable transactions more often than they have unprofitable ones. But the rules of the New York Stock Exchange require that the public interest must come first. That's why all specialists have to meet high standards of market experience, capital (twenty trading units of a stock is the minimum allowed, but many specialists own far more), and character, and their activities are subject to constant scrutiny by the Exchange and the SEC.

You will remember that we said earlier that the financial world operates according to the law of supply and demand — but that law isn't always allowed to work without some interference. The function of the specialist is a good example of that "interference" in a good cause. It is because of the specialist that when a buyer wants to buy, there is always a seller; and when a seller wants to sell, there is always a buyer — regardless of the amount of public interest in a stock at the moment. And it is because of the specialist that stock prices do not fluctuate as much as they might in a completely unregulated market.

19.

How New Securities Come to Market

So far we've talked mostly about buying securities that have been traded for a while either in the over-the-counter market or on the floor of one of the exchanges. You may be wondering how those securities came into existence. We touched on that subject briefly when we talked about the expansion of Jackson Bakery. Now let's go into more detail.

Raising Funds

Let's say that Red, White & Blue Corporation needs money to build a new plant. The first step is probably to call in an investment banker, also known as an underwriter. An investment banker is neither a banker in the usual sense nor a person. It is a firm that serves as a middle man between corporations that want to obtain funds for expansion and development and the investing public. Many brokerage houses are investment banking firms as well.

The officers of Red, White & Blue may call in one investment banking firm and negotiate an arrangement with that firm to offer securities to the public. Or it may call in several investment bankers and ask them to bid competitively for the opportunity of offering the corporation's securities to the public, with the highest bidder winning the right to market the issue. (Red, White & Blue naturally wants to get as much money as possible for its securities.) Somewhere along the way, a decision has been made as to whether Red, White & Blue will borrow money (that is, issue bonds) or increase its number of owners (that is, sell stock). If Red, White & Blue has been privately owned and is now selling securities to the general public for the first time, the company is said to be *going public*.

What Red, White & Blue is trying to do by issuing securities is clear enough: It is simply raising money. But what is the objective of the investment banking firm? The investment banker hopes to make money by buying the whole issue of new securities from Red, White & Blue and then selling those securities to the investing public — both individuals and institutions — at a higher price, say 5 percent to 10 percent higher. That 5 percent to 10 percent, which is called a spread, is not pure profit. Out of it the investment banker must pay all expenses involved in the sale of the new securities. And those expenses may be considerable.

Spreading the Risk

A very large issue of new securities may be too much for one investment banking firm to handle. The issue may represent more money than the investment banker is able to buy or wishes to commit at one time. In that case, the investment banker may invite other investment banking firms to join an underwriting group to share the risk, the work, and the profit. Then the original investment banking firm usually acts as manager and "runs the books" (does the paper work), and each of the other investment banking firms in the underwriting group agrees to take a certain portion of the new issue and sell it to investors.

Holding the Line

The public offering price of a new issue of stock is set shortly before the stock goes on sale and depends on market conditions as well as on such things as Red, White & Blue's past earnings and future prospects. All the members of the underwriting group and the selling syndicate (if there is one) agree to sell the new issue at that price for a certain period of time — sometimes as little as a day, sometimes as much as a few weeks. Initially, the stock will be offered to the public at a net price, without commission. And once the stock is in the hands of investors, its price will fluctuate in accordance with investors' opinions of it.

The new issue may be bonds instead of stock, of course. In fact, in dollar figures, more new bonds than new stocks are sold most years. Most bonds are bought by institutional investors rather than by individuals. The face value of a bond is usually $1,000, but before a bond is offered for sale, the corporation and the investment banker must reach decisions about maturity, interest rate, and whether the bonds will be offered at par, at a discount, or at a premium — decisions that depend to some extent on the behavior of the market and the tightness of money at the time.

Meeting the Requirements

At last the new issue of securities is ready to be sold to the public. Or is it? If the issue is worth $300,000 or more, the company must register it with the SEC, which involves supplying the SEC with all kinds of information about the company and its financial situation. The company must also prepare a booklet called a prospectus, containing pertinent financial information, and a copy of the preliminary prospectus is given to everyone involved in the underwriting and selling of the securities and to everyone who indicates an interest in buying the securities. The SEC requires a prospectus to be sure that the facts and figures that an investor should know are made available to him before he buys the security. The prospectus is usually prepared by a team of representatives of the corporation, its lawyers, and representatives of the investment banking firm, and it follows a certain pattern.

Actually, two prospectuses are usually prepared. The first one is called a *red herring* just because it contains, printed in red on the cover, some words of warning that the information inside is subject to completion or amendment. The offering price of the security is also missing because it hasn't been set yet. It is the last thing to be decided and depends on market conditions at the time of the offering. Copies of the red herring are distributed by the investment banker to underwriters who may participate in the underwriting and securities dealers who may sell the securities to the public and to interested investors.

The SEC reviews the company's registration statement and the preliminary prospectus and eventually — after a few weeks or several months, depending on the complexity of the company's financial situation and the number of other new issues which the SEC must review — allows the issue to be offered to the public *if* the data seem complete and honest. The SEC does not pass judgment on the investment quality of the security; it merely allows or does not allow the issue to be offered to the public.

Paper Tombstones

Once the SEC has given the green light, the investment banking firm which is managing the offering places an advertisement in the financial pages of a newspaper. The advertisement contains only the bare facts about the new security: the name of the issue, its price, its size (number of shares), and the names of the underwriters, from whom interested investors can obtain prospectuses. This kind of advertisement is set in a very simple and dignified style and is known in Wall Street as a *tombstone*. The final prospectus is ready to be issued by this time, and it contains the offering price, which was missing from the red herring.

NEW ISSUE.

June 4, 1968

500,000 Shares

Red, White & Blue Corporation

Common Stock
($1 Par Value)

Price $10 per Share

Copies of the Prospectus may be obtained in any State in which this announcement is circulated from only such of the undersigned or other dealers or brokers as may lawfully offer these securities in such State.

Broker A

Broker B   **Broker C**   **Broker D**   **Broker E**

A so-called tombstone advertisement for a new issue of securities.
COURTESY OF MERRILL LYNCH, PIERCE, FENNER & SMITH INC.

Once in a Lifetime

Let's assume that Red, White & Blue's new issue of common stock has managed to get over all these hurdles, and the issue is finally offered to the investing public. The new issue may be sold out (by brokers to their customers) in a matter of minutes, or it may take the selling group weeks to find buyers. Generally speaking, this is the only time in the life of the stock when the price is set. It is set by agreement between the corporation and the investment banker. But once the stock is in public hands, its price will fluctuate, reflecting people's opinion of the company's prospects — and the old law of supply and demand. For forty days, the only information available about the company will be the prospectus. No broker is allowed to publicize the stock in any other way. That's another SEC regulation.

Red, White & Blue receives a check from the investment banking firm for the amount of the new issue of securities and has the funds it needs for a new plant. The underwriters and sellers have played their parts as middle men between the company and the public, and they receive their portion of the spread between what the company received and the public paid for the securities. And the investing public has increased its stake in American industry.

In addition to the federal regulations regarding new issues of securities, many states have their own laws designed to protect investors from fraud. Those laws, which vary from state to state, are generally called *blue-sky laws,* probably because they were passed to keep dishonest salesmen from selling securities worth as much as a patch of blue sky. Before a new issue of securities can be offered to people living in states with blue-sky laws, a prospectus containing financial information about the company must be filed with the appropriate state authorities — just one more instance of the protection of the investor by the law.

You may be wondering why the SEC keeps such a watchful eye on new issues of securities. The purpose is to make sure that investors have all the important facts and figures about a company before they make investment decisions and at the same time to protect investors from some of the abuses of earlier years, such as watered stock, stock that was sold to the public at a certain price and appeared on the company's records at a higher price, thus making the company look more prosperous than it was.

Rights

A corporation that has already gone public and that is issuing new stock often gives its present stockholders a chance to buy the new stock to add to their holdings. The company does so by issuing what are called *subscription rights,* or simply rights, offering the stock for a limited period of time at a price that is considerably below the market price of the stock already in public hands at that time. The reason for doing this is to enable the stockholder to continue to own the same proportionate share of the company's stock if he wishes to do so. The rights have a market value, and if the stockholder chooses not to use or exercise them himself, he can have his broker sell them for him.

20.

People Who Work in the Securities Business

Nobody knows exactly how many people work in the securities business all over the country. The New York Stock Exchange estimates the number of employees of member firms of the Exchange at over 100,000, and that does not include employees of other exchanges, over-the-counter dealers, and mutual funds. All that can be said for certain is that the people who work in the securities business are numerous enough to populate a sizable city. But of course they are not all concentrated in one place. Some are on LaSalle Street in Chicago, some on Montgomery Street in San Francisco, others are scattered across the country in all the sizable cities. A substantial number of them work in the Wall Street area of New York — "the street," as it is sometimes called — simply because Wall Street is the headquarters for much of the securities business.

The Registered Rep

The only member of the widely scattered financial community that most investors ever meet is the registered representative of a brokerage house, who may also be called an account executive or a customers' man (although that term smacks somewhat of the old days before the regulation of the securities business) but who is generally known to his customers as "my broker."

A broker is likely to spend a large part of his working day on the telephone at his desk in a brokerage-house board room and some time talking in person with customers who drop in to see him or whom he calls on in their homes or offices. His function, after all, is to sell securities. But, unlike other salesmen, he is required to know his customer and his customer's circumstances and needs and not to sell him anything that is not consistent with those circumstances and needs. And that makes him a rather special kind of salesman.

A broker keeps up with the market at all times in a variety of ways: by reading the ticker, using his quotation equipment, reading various financial publications (especially *The Wall Street Journal*) and reports of financial information services and materials prepared by his own company's research department, attending briefing sessions designed to keep him posted on market developments, and searching out investment ideas and information wherever he can find them. He is a gatherer

185

A broker at work in his office in a brokerage house board room.
PHOTO BY ROY STEVENS, COURTESY OF MERRILL LYNCH, PIERCE, FENNER &
SMITH INC.

and dispenser of investment ideas from a great number of sources, forever busy because the market is forever changing and making his information and opinions obsolete. Most brokers do "homework," too — reading financial news in newspapers and magazines, annual reports, material from the financial information services, and anything else that will keep them better informed and better able to help their customers. Some brokers also teach courses in investing in local night schools and give talks about investing before local groups.

Most of the approximately 42,000 registered representatives in the United States are men, although there are a few women brokers. If there is such a thing as a typical broker, he is probably a college graduate in his thirties or forties, married and with a family, living comfortably in or near a fairly large city. What all registered representatives have in common is that they have studied their business either in the training school of one of the larger member firms or in a correspondence course and have passed the qualifying examinations given and required by the New York Stock Exchange.

Behind the Scenes

There are, of course, many men and women in the securities business whom the general public never meets face to face. Among them are the men who work on the floors of the exchanges (See Chapter 16), those who are active in the investment-banking or underwriting part of the business (See Chapter 19), and the traders through whom all securities that are traded over the counter change hands, including government and municipal and corporate bonds and many common stocks (See Chapters 5 and 7).

Most brokerage houses have research departments, too,

187

where men and women (usually known as security analysts) study the market as a whole and various industries and individual companies by reading about them, talking with company officers, visiting factories and laboratories, and collecting information wherever they can to enable them to size up companies' investment prospects. The information they collect and the opinions they form are used in a variety of ways to increase their firm's business, and some of it is relayed to the firm's registered representatives to help keep them informed and to enable them to serve their customers well. The research departments of some firms issue periodic market letters for their customers, and some of them publish reports and booklets which are available to the general public. You may occasionally see the letters C.F.A. after the name of a security analyst. The letters stand for Chartered Financial Analyst and mean that the person has taken and passed a series of examinations given by the Financial Analysts Federation, which sets standards for the professional practice of financial analysis.

Some of the larger brokerage houses offer to help investors and prospective investors by suggesting investments and reviewing portfolios (*portfolio* is a two-dollar word for holdings, the securities that a person owns) free of charge. Such suggestions and reviews are usually prepared by portfolio analysts, who have for their use not only the information and opinions of the firm's security analysts but also their own knowledge of how to balance risk and return, of pertinent tax factors, of economic conditions and trends. It is the portfolio analyst's job to try to tailor investments to the individual investor's needs. But the analyst does not buy or sell securities. He merely suggests. If the person who requested investment suggestions or a portfolio review chooses to act on the recommendations of the portfolio analyst, it is the firm's registered representative who takes the orders and sees that they are executed.

There are, of course, many other people working behind the scenes in the securities business — people involved in executing orders and recording information for confirmations and statements and handling money and certificates and sending mail to customers and handling correspondence and doing countless other essential jobs that the public knows nothing about.

Enter the Computer

The population of the financial community has grown tremendously in the past ten years. And so has the "population" of computers. It is not an exaggeration to say that Wall Street could not cope with the heavy volume of trading in securities — a record 2.5 billion shares on the New York Stock Exchange in 1967, a record 1.1 billion shares on the American Stock Exchange, and enormous totals also on other exchanges and in the over-the-counter market — if it were not for computers. When 10,000,000 shares of stock change hands on the New York Stock Exchange alone on an average day and every bit of paper work in connection with every transaction is supposed to be completed before the next day's trading starts, you can imagine that there simply are not enough clerks to handle the work without the help of computers for speedy recording and calculating and printing. Gone are the days when visored clerks sitting at high, sloping desks recorded trades in giant ledgers in a fine Spencerian hand. They may have been picturesque, but they could never have kept up with the pace of trading in the 1960's. The computer has proved to be a great blessing to Wall

189

Street, and far from doing away with jobs, it has created many more by increasing the capacity of brokerage firms in many directions and enabling them not only to cope with the volume of trading but also to expand their operations.

At first, computers were used chiefly to streamline the handling of payrolls, then transactions, then margin accounts. Today computers are used for many other operations, including research. Because they can retrieve and sort information and make calculations with great speed and accuracy, security analysts and portfolio analysts have found them invaluable to perform tasks that would take thousands of man hours. The computer relieves them of many routine jobs and gives them more time for interpretation, theorizing, questioning, and problem-solving.

Research is only one place where computers are making their mark in the securities business. Every aspect of the business is feeling their impact — and will feel it even more strongly in the future. It is the computer that makes possible the up-to-the-second quotations on securities that you can get in almost any broker's office. Computers are used to compute the various averages that tell you how the market is behaving at any given time. Computers made possible the University of Chicago study of rates of return on common stocks which determined that from 1926 to 1960, the average rate of return on listed common stocks before taxes was 9 percent compounded annually and that three out of every four sales were profitable. And finally, the computer now enables the SEC to scrutinize the trading in the stock market more carefully than ever before, to detect abuses almost as soon as they happen, and to take any action that may be necessary to put an end to them at once.

21.

Who's Looking Over Your Broker's Shoulder?

When you buy securities, how can you be sure that you won't be cheated in some way? The answer to that not unreasonable question is that there are dishonest people in every business, including the securities business, but it is hard for them to succeed in cheating investors because the securities business is one of the most highly regulated businesses in the world. It is regulated by federal and state laws, and it is self-regulated as well.

What kinds of regulations and agencies are there to protect investors?

The First Act

The first of the federal laws to be passed was the Securities Act of 1933, which is also known as the "Truth-in-Securities Act." It required, for the first time, full disclosure in a registration statement of all material facts about any new issue of securities worth more than $300,000 that was offered to the public. And it further required that a prospectus containing those facts be sent with any offer of the securities by a dealer to a customer for forty days after the registration or ninety days if it was the company's first registration. The law prohibited misstatements and set penalties for the distribution of false information by mail. Neither that law nor any other can protect an investor from his own bad judgment, but at least it assures him that complete and accurate information about a new security is available to help him make up his mind whether to buy it or not. The Securities Act of 1933 was in some respects merely an extension of the so-called blue-sky laws of various states, many of which were on the books before 1933.

The Second Act

The Securities Act of 1933, which regulated new issues of securities, was followed by the more extensive federal Securities Exchange Act of 1934, which was designed to regulate the so-called *aftermarket,* the market for securities already in public hands. To regulate the securities markets, the Act created the Securities and Exchange Commission, a government agency composed of five men, not more than three of whom can be from one political party. As we mentioned earlier, members of the SEC are appointed by the President with the advice and consent of the Senate, and they serve rotating five-year terms. Responsibility for the regulation of speculative credit — margin buying and short selling — was divided between the Securities and Exchange Commission (SEC) and the Federal Reserve Board (FRB). And the securities industry was charged with policing itself in many ways.

Among the provisions of the Securities Exchange Act of 1934 are these: registration of securities exchanges (which are required to file their constitutions, rules of procedure, and provisions for disciplining violators), of their members, and of securities listed on them; prohibition of manipulative practices — that is, forcing stock prices up and down for purposes of fraud; and the sending of accurate proxy statements to stockholders. The act requires the licensing of registered representatives, who must pass examinations designed to test their knowledge of the business before they can do business with the public.

Two amendments later in the 1930's provided for the registration of brokers and dealers in the over-the-counter market and for the creation of the National Association of Securities Dealers to police that market.

The SEC: Who and What?

The SEC, which has its headquarters in Washington and eleven other offices scattered around the country, keeps its eye on every aspect of the securities business. It watches the day-to-day and minute-to-minute activities in both the listed markets and the over-the-counter market for evidence of manipulation or any other illegal activity. It oversees the registration and regulation of investment companies. It requires sizable companies (assets over $1 million, more than 500 stockholders) with stocks traded over the counter to report regularly to the SEC and to their stockholders in the manner of listed companies. And it investigates accusations of dishonest dealing among brokers. For example, a registered representative who is found guilty of churning, of trying to generate an unsuitable amount in commissions from one of his accounts, will be penalized by the SEC, and his whole firm may be implicated if there is evidence that the firm either encouraged the activity or was too casual about its supervision.

The SEC has it in its power to suspend an exchange or suspend trading in a security or suspend the registration of a broker or dealer. Since a suspension means no income for those suspended, it may have serious consequences. The SEC can also prevent violations of the law by means of injunctions and prosecute those guilty of serious violations by criminal action.

In short, the SEC is constantly on the lookout for any evidence that securities firms are favoring themselves over the public or taking advantage of the public in any way. Behind the SEC's activities is a theory called the shingle theory, which says that when a broker hangs out his shingle, he guarantees that he will deal fairly with his customers. There is, of course, some difference of opinion about what constitutes fairness, but the SEC is not known for its easy-going attitude. It is not only demanding but exacting in its scrutiny of the securities business.

The Money Market

We mentioned the FRB in connection with speculative credit. The FRB, more accurately the Board of Governors of the Fed-

194

eral Reserve System, is a group of seven men appointed by the President (who designates one of the seven as chairman) and confirmed by the Senate for terms of fourteen years each. The terms rotate, one expiring every two years, so the composition of the FRB changes every two years. The chief responsibility of the FRB is directing the operations of the Federal Reserve System of twelve Federal Reserve banks, but the Board also controls United States monetary policy in a variety of ways. It sets the discount rate, the rate at which commercial banks can borrow from the Federal Reserve System; it buys and sells government securities in the open market, thus affecting the amount of money in circulation at any given time; it determines reserve requirements of banks, an activity which also affects the availability of money and the interest rates that money will command; and, as we know, it sets initial margin requirements. It is the FRB that decides whether margin buyers and short sellers have to put up all of the money for their activities or only part of it, depending on the amount of speculation in the securities markets and on general financial conditions in the country.

Enter the New York Stock Exchange

It may seem strange, but the FRB does not regulate margin buying and short selling after the original transaction in a stock. Margin maintenance, the proportion of stock that a speculator must own, is set by rules of the New York Stock Exchange and by brokers themselves. The New York Stock Exchange, as we have seen, is regulated by the SEC. And in turn, it regulates its own activities and those of its members. Its rules, in fact, are so extensive as to fill a whole book. In previous chapters, we discussed some of the rules of the New York

Stock Exchange regarding membership, the activities of specialists, requirements for listing, and activities on the trading floor. Among the New York Stock Exchange's other policing activities are these: regulation of commissions charged by member firms (the SEC oversees this also), administration of qualifying examinations for registered representatives, and regulation of all advertising by member firms.

Since 1964, the Exchange has had a $25,000,000 fund to cover the possible insolvency of any member firm which is likely to hurt that firm's customers or investors in general. In other words, if a member firm goes broke and investors are likely to lose money as a result, the Exchange has a fund from which it can "make the customers whole" if necessary.

Behind all of the New York Stock Exchange's rules lies one rule for all member firms and their registered representatives: Know your customer. Partly for his own protection (since the customer may be dishonest) but mostly for the customer's protection, each registered representative is supposed to know the financial condition and the objectives of each of his customers so that he can help them find investments to suit their circumstances. So when you open an account with a broker, if he seems to ask a lot of personal questions, he is only following the rules of the business and trying to help you as much as possible. He is not just being a nosy-parker.

. . . and the NASD

The NASD has a similar suitability rule which states that brokers and dealers in the over-the-counter market must make their investment suggestions conform to their customers' needs. The NASD — short for National Association of Securities Dealers — is responsible to the SEC and regulates the over-the-

196

counter market in a variety of ways. Applicants to be registered representatives must pass its qualifying examination. The NASD supplies daily quotations to the wire services and newspapers and attempts to enforce the rule that limits markups to 5 percent. The NASD administers the policy that restricts investment-company advertising and promotion material to statements of facts and records of performance — minus big promises of future performance. And it has the authority to discipline, censure, fine, suspend, or expel any of its 3,700 members who violate its rules or those of the SEC.

More important than any rules or regulatory agencies is the character of the men and women in the industry. There are scoundrels and opportunists and weaklings in every field of endeavor. But the securities business is so hard on those who violate its rules, written and unwritten, that fair dealing prevails perhaps more than it does in most other kinds of business.

22.

Conclusion

We've said that the reason for buying stocks and bonds is to make money — more money than you can make by your own efforts alone and more than you can make by letting your money lie idle instead of working for you. But there's more to investing than that.

Investing is a way of participating in our country's future. Not all of us are gifted in ways which may enable us to harness the power of the sun, discover how to grow crops under the sea to feed hungry nations, find a cure for cancer, or develop ways of controlling air and water pollution.

But that doesn't mean we must stand on the sidelines. We can get involved by putting our surplus money to work where it will be used to good effect, by risking our capital where the prospects look most promising and where the rewards appear greatest in terms of accomplishment and satisfaction as well as profit.

Capitalism is just as much a part of the American way of life as are free speech and due process of law. And it is your privilege as a citizen of the United States to enjoy *all* the advantages that citizenship affords.

GLOSSARY OF STREET TALK

Every business has a language all its own, and the securities business is no exception. You've undoubtedly encountered some new words while reading this book, and here are some others that haven't been defined and that you're sure to find in the financial pages of your newspaper or in talking with a broker. In alphabetical order:

Appreciation. In Wall Street, appreciation is not a feeling of gratitude for a favor. It means price appreciation, an increase in the value of a stock.

200

Blue chip. The term blue chip comes from poker, where the blue chips are the most valuable chips. In Wall Street, the term refers to common stocks of high quality in large and well-known companies such as American Telephone & Telegraph, General Electric, and International Business Machines Corporation.

Broad tape. A typical brokerage office has a Dow-Jones teletype machine that carries news that is likely to affect the stock market. It is called the broad tape to distinguish it from ticker tape, which is narrow (three-quarters of an inch).

Bull and bear. Bulls and bears aren't animals; they're people. A bull is a person who thinks the market, or a particular stock, is going to go up, and a bear thinks the market or a stock is going to go down. You might say that a bull is an optimist and a bear is a pessimist.

Cats and dogs. These aren't animals, either, nor are they people. They are very speculative stocks of doubtful quality and are best avoided.

Closed corporation. A closed corporation is a company whose stock is owned by a small group of people, sometimes the members of a family, and is not available to the general public.

Conglomerate. The conglomerate corporation has become more and more common in recent years. It is a group of several companies in different businesses making up one corporation. Sometimes a conglomerate comes into existence to enable an older corporation to move into a fast-growing business by buying a company already in that business instead of starting from scratch, sometimes representing an effort to give a company a shot in the arm. Among the well-known conglomerates, companies engaged in a variety of different businesses, are Gulf & Western Industries, International Telephone & Telegraph, L-T-V, Litton Industries, and Textron.

Corner. You might think corner refers to where Wall and Broad streets meet in lower Manhattan, where the New York Stock Exchange is. But the meaning is more like cornering a wild animal in a place from which he can't escape. To corner the market means to buy up all the available supply of stock in a company and thus to make it impossible for short sellers to borrow the shares they need to make delivery. Corners are illegal now, but they used to be fairly common in the nineteenth and early twentieth centuries.

Correction. When stock prices move temporarily against the prevailing trend, a correction is said to have taken place. Most often the word is used when the market has been going up and prices suddenly drop. If prices drop and then rise again, a rally is said to have taken place.

Curb. Curb is the nickname of the American Stock Exchange, because it used to be outdoors on Wall Street and Broad Street — on the curb or sidewalk. It has been indoors since 1921.

Cut a melon. In Wall Street, a melon isn't food; it's an extra dividend because a company has had an unusually prosperous year. When the directors of a company vote an extra dividend, they are said to cut a melon.

Equity. Equities are stocks, both common and preferred.

Fall out of bed. When stock prices take a sudden drop, they are said to have fallen out of bed.

Gilt-edged securities. Gilt-edged securities are high-quality bonds. The term probably originated in the days when bond certificates had gold edges. Those days are gone forever.

Give-up order. Suppose you have an account with brokerage house A, and you are visiting a city where A has no office at a time when you decide you want to sell some of your stock. You can, of course, telephone your order by long distance to your registered representative. But you can also go into the office of brokerage house B in the city you are visiting, give the name of your regular broker, identify yourself, and place your order. B will handle the transaction for you, and B and A will split the commission. Then B is said to give up part of the commission to A.

Insider. Insiders are officers, directors, and large stockholders of corporations. They often have inside information about their companies' financial affairs, and they are forbidden to use it for their own financial advantage. They are also required to report any change in the amount of their holdings of their companies' stock to the SEC and, if the company is listed, to the New York Stock Exchange. That information is published periodically in *The Wall Street Journal* and elsewhere for the information of investors.

Killing. To make a killing is what every speculator dreams of doing. It means to sell a stock at a large profit after holding it only a short time.

Liquidate. Liquidate does not mean kill in Wall Street. It means to sell your holdings, to turn them into cash. A security that can be sold readily (such as a Treasury bill) is said to be liquid.

Long. If you are long a security, you own that security. To be short is to have sold a stock you didn't own and borrowed it to make delivery, as explained in Chapter 10.

Narrow market, thin market. A stock that has a narrow market is one that trades in a very small price range — just a few points. A stock has a thin market when there is a relatively small number of shares in the hands of investors.

Play the market. This is an unfortunate term that makes investing sound easy. It means buying and selling frequently in the hope of making a profit.

Secondary. Secondary is short for secondary distribution, which means a sale of a large block of stock, most of which is already in public hands. A primary distribution is the sale of stock to the public for the first time (as described in Chapter 19), and a secondary distribution is any large sale after the first one.

Take a bath. In Wall Street, taking a bath is what nobody ever wants to do. It means losing money heavily, "going to the cleaners."

Tip. In Wall Street, a tip isn't money given for good service. It is a piece of information that is supposed to indicate that a stock will soon rise or fall, and the recipient of the information is presumably in a position to profit. Beware of tips. They are usually handed out for the benefit of the one who is giving the information, not the one who is receiving it.

Treasury stock. It sounds as if this ought to be stock in the United States Treasury, but the Treasury doesn't issue stock — only various kinds of bonds. Treasury stock is a company's own stock which the company holds in its treasury instead of selling it to the public. It may be held to pay bonuses to employees or to allow executives to buy shares at desirable prices as part of an incentive plan. Treasury stock has no voting rights or dividend rights, but it it is sold to the public, it gains those rights.

* * *

Now you know why some 24,000,000 Americans own securities. But why securities instead of some other kind of investment? After all, they might have bought real estate or art or jewels, which may also tend to increase in value through the years. But one needs very special knowledge to make such investments, and help and advice are not so readily available as they are if you wish to buy securities. Then, too, there is the question of liquidity, of being able to turn an investment into cash at will. If you need cash and own real estate, art, or jewels, it may take you quite a while to sell them and get your money. But securities can be sold readily for cash at any time.

INDEX